How Did I Get to Be
70 When I'm
35 Inside?

Spiritual Surprises of *Later Life*

Linda Douty

Walking Together, Finding the Way ®
SKYLIGHT PATHS®
PUBLISHING
Woodstock, Vermont

How Did I Get to Be 70 When I'm 35 Inside?
Spiritual Surprises of Later Life

2013 Quality Paperback Edition, Third Printing

Grateful acknowledgment is given for permission to use material from the following sources: The poem "Sorrow" by Judy Sorum Brown is reprinted by permission of the author. The excerpt from the chapter "Gratitude and Ambiguity" of *God Is an Amateur* by John R. Claypool, copyright © 1994 by Forward Movement, is used by permission of Forward Movement. The poem "The Invitation" by Oriah Mountain Dreamer, from her book *The Invitation* © 1999, published by HarperOne, San Francisco, is presented with permission of the author. All rights reserved. www.oriah.org.

Library of Congress Cataloging-in-Publication Data
Douty, Linda.
   How did I get to be 70 when I'm 35 inside? : spiritual surprises of later life / Linda Douty. — Quality paperback ed.
      p. cm.
   Includes bibliographical references.
   ISBN 978-1-59473-297-3 (pbk.)
   1. Aging—Religious aspects—Christianity. 2. Aging—Psychological aspects. 3.
Aging—Social aspects. I. Title.
   BV4580.D64 2011
   248.8'5—dc22
                                                                    2011004750

10 9 8 7 6 5 4 3
Manufactured in the United States of America

Cover Design: Jenny Buono
Cover Art: Adult Hen © Eric Isselée / iStockphoto.com; Baby Chick © Nicholas / iStockphoto.com
Interior Design: Kristi Menter

SkyLight Paths Publishing is creating a place where people of different spiritual traditions come together for challenge and inspiration, a place where we can help each other understand the mystery that lies at the heart of our existence.

SkyLight Paths sees both believers and seekers as a community that increasingly transcends traditional boundaries of religion and denomination—people wanting to learn from each other, *walking together, finding the way.*®

SkyLight Paths, "Walking Together, Finding the Way" and colophon are trademarks of LongHill Partners, Inc., registered in the U.S. Patent and Trademark Office.

Walking Together, Finding the Way®
Published by SkyLight Paths Publishing
A Division of LongHill Partners, Inc.
Sunset Farm Offices, Route 4, P.O. Box 237
Woodstock, VT 05091
Tel: (802) 457-4000   Fax: (802) 457-4004
www.skylightpaths.com

On the other hand, a growing sense of self makes your appearance seem less important. Here's a side of another coin: there may be a loss of identity when familiar roles fade. On the other is the bonus of no longer having to rush to the office to make a buck or rush to get the kids to school. In this book, I'll look at both sides of the coin of aging—stark reality as well as optimism.

Here's the way the book unfolds: Before we can reflect on the significance of surprise, a certain degree of openness is essential. So, chapter 1 deals with the courage necessary to notice surprises. It suggests ways we can accept and flow, rather than resist and congeal.

The first group of surprises centers around the emergence of the Authentic Self, as we let go of the burdens of the younger self-image—baggage that was packed for us by parents, culture, media, and religion. Next we'll explore surprises that the body presents, those we can control and those we can't. Relationships change also, as children grow up, friends move away, and the old roles no longer fit. Surprises in the realm of the sacred deal with the impact of religion and faith on this stage of life. The final three chapters report on the specific challenges, gifts, and wisdom passed along from these seasoned seniors to you, the reader. So this won't be a book about how you *ought* to grow older, but rather a candid report on what it's really like and some new ways of thinking about it.

Look at it this way: No one has ever won the fierce battle against aging, though many a skirmish has been fought. But the meaning emerges and the fun begins when you put down your sword.

Linda Douty
Memphis, Tennessee

- What have you discovered about yourself that you didn't know before?
- How has your image of God changed as you age? Your thoughts about life after death?
- What dreams have you buried?
- How have you coped with physical limitations without becoming boring or bitter?
- What has been your greatest challenge in aging? Your greatest joy?
- How old do you feel *inside*? How old are you *outside*?

I encouraged them to express what they *actually* felt, rather than what they were *supposed* to feel. The discussions sparked by these questions produced such intriguing insights that I scrapped my original outline and started over. My usual approach to writing had been to decide what I wanted to say, organize a structure (table of contents), and then flesh it out. But these folks between the ages of seventy and ninety-nine kept giving me answers that I didn't expect, and it soon became obvious that there was no "one size fits all," even within the same gender. Their ideas about aging were as unique as their personalities. Threads of wisdom began to emerge from their thoughtful reflections. To be honest, this is the first time I have allowed a book to be born on its own terms without my micromanagement.

The word "surprise" kept inadvertently popping up in our conversations. As the interviewees talked about things that surprised them, I began to get in touch with what was surprising me in my own process of aging. Along the way, I was reminded that the word *surprise* is essentially neutral. It doesn't always carry the aura of delight normally associated with the concept. It merely means "unexpected." You can be surprised by an inheritance from Aunt Gertrude or by a cancer diagnosis during a routine physical exam.

The maturing process itself carries this same kind of unpredictability. As in all of life, there are at least two sides of the coin. On the one hand, the body's natural decline begins to show itself.

an athlete, nip and tuck like a starlet, be incessantly positive, and stay busy. But those answers don't fit the deeper needs of later life.

Because I have a stubborn tendency to view everything through rose-colored glasses, I made a firm decision to approach this stage of life with a smile and a shrug. But my body and my contemporaries were saying, "Not so fast, Pollyanna—this ain't all a bed of roses!" So I decided to get real. After all, later life presents life's grandest opportunity for honesty.

I began to notice other changes besides the obvious wrinkles. There were invisible issues underneath the visible ones—unspoken fears, unthinkable losses, deserted dreams, and a free-floating anxiety about how and when I will die—all spiritual conundrums that emerge as time grows shorter. In contrast, surprising satisfactions and unexpected pleasures were also a part of the package. New questions bubbled up: Did men and women differ in their reactions to aging? Did their faith journeys make a difference? Did their relationship with God change? How did awareness of death affect value systems, not to mention their relationships with themselves and others?

In the work of spiritual direction—both receiving and giving in this special relationship—I've found that the spiritual self is inseparable from the physical body, the workings of the mind, and behavior in the workplace, the home, and the world. Every thought, action, and life event has a spiritual component. So no matter whether the name of God is mentioned or not, the Spirit moves through our lives and, I hope, through the pages of this book.

I decided to get outside my own head to see what others were experiencing. Over a period of a few months, more than fifty articulate seniors agreed to respond to some pretty nosy questions (with a guarantee of confidentiality, of course):

- What has surprised you most about aging?
- Is there something about growing older that you've never said out loud?

Introduction

This is the book I have longed to write. The seed was planted one spring day while sitting in my favorite rocking chair, routinely checking the daily mail. The postman had delivered two significant envelopes; the synchronicity was both startling and just plain funny.

In one hand was my new Medicare card with its twin messages: yes, I was sixty-five, the official beginning of old age as recognized by the U.S. government; and yes, I was being given a "raise," because my hefty health-insurance premiums would virtually disappear.

In the other hand was the edited manuscript of my first book, written at the ripe old age of sixty-four. The obvious paradox brought a smile to my face. In one hand was a symbol of the "beginning of the end," and in the other the "beginning of a beginning." I used to think that age sixty-five was the start of a slippery downward slope to the cemetery. But inside, I felt a surge of enormous energy, with the potential to approach aging as an uncharted adventure instead of a prison sentence.

Five years have elapsed since that memorable day. Unexpected events have challenged me physically, financially, emotionally, and spiritually. I've read a shelf-full of books telling me how to grow old gracefully—most of them with specific instructions on how to hold the appearance of Father Time at bay—eat like a bird, work out like

*To my dear sisters, Anita and Mickey,
my companions through all the stages of life,
... especially this last one.*

Integrity is the ability to listen to a place inside oneself that
doesn't change, even though the life that carries it may
change.
JONATHAN OMER-MAN

Contents

Opening to Surprise

Every tomorrow has two doors; we can enter through the door of resistance or the door of growth. The first is fueled by fear, the second by faith.

W hat have you noticed about your aging patients?" I asked with interest.

The three doctors of internal medicine paused thoughtfully before they responded. There were two men and one woman, ranging in age from forty to seventy, all with a large number of elderly patients in their thriving medical practices. I knew they would have years of experience in observing a host of reactions from actual patients, so I invited them to share their collective wisdom about aging. In exchange for my guarantee of anonymity for them and their patients, they agreed not to sugarcoat anything or pull any punches.

Two Doors

As they offered opinions and stories, some common themes began to emerge. One doctor summed it up in these words: "It's like this," he began. "As people age, they tend to move in one of two directions, one that looks backward and one that looks forward."

"That's too simplistic," his colleague insisted. "I think it's as if one group is invested in the status quo and holds on to the familiar. The others let go of what isn't working and are willing to change, even if they don't know exactly what that change is going to look like."

I urged them to be more specific. "How do those two directions look in the lives of real people? What are the signs that someone is moving toward one path or the other?" Their descriptions were revealing. Challenging, too. (I wanted to do a quick self-inventory to see which doorway I was heading toward.) Of course, most of us share a mixture of these two directions. Maybe on an "up" day, we tend more toward growth; on a "down" day, we might have our feet stuck in resistance. Still, we probably show dominance in one of these two basic points of view.

Door One—Resistance
- Those who repeatedly refer to "the good old days."
- Those who are unwilling to consider ideas that differ from their own.
- Those who seem categorically opposed to change, championing the status quo.
- Those who whine and complain, wanting medication to fix whatever ails them—*right now*.
- Those who are unwilling to examine old patterns of communication and behavior.
- Those who are unwilling to examine their religious beliefs and deal with reasonable doubts.
- Those who tend to take advantage of physical limitation, making it an excuse not to grow.
- Those who are "set in their ways."

Door Two—Growth
- Those who are curious about learning.
- Those who are eager to discover who they truly are, apart from cultural expectations.

- Those who are committed to more honesty in their relationships.
- Those who challenge old patterns to test their validity for the present.
- Those who accept what is, rather than complain about it.
- Those who can adapt to loss and are willing to change their lives in harmony with their change in circumstances, look honestly at what they are holding on to, and identify barriers to their own growth.
- Those who find the courage to tackle the work of letting go.
- Those who move from the tyranny of "I ought to" to the freedom of "I choose to."

The doctors agreed that the pattern of loss and gain weaves its way through the entire aging process and needs to be confronted consciously. Studies show that folks who age in healthy ways are more realistic about the staggering array of late-life losses, which range from the trivial to the tragic. They intentionally nurture their souls and develop new skills to deal with the inevitable changes honestly. They stare the losses and gains right in the face:

- They bid goodbye to waistlines and say hello to wrinkles.
- They lose people they love through death and divorce and have to reinvent themselves without those relationships.
- They retire from meaningful vocations and roles, facing the question, "What now?"
- They discover their religious faith may be little more than a collection of habits and unexamined beliefs, and they want to experience faith as reality, not just religion.

- They want to connect with their essential core—the real Me apart from the roles they play.

Will these conundrums break us open or break us down? Episcopal priest and author Cynthia Bourgeault describes our responses in terms of yielding or bracing when we are confronted with either a negative threat or a positive opportunity:

> You will notice yourself responding in one of two ways. Either you will brace, harden, and resist, or you will soften, open, and yield. If you go with the former gesture, you will be catapulted immediately into your smaller self, with its animal instincts and survival responses. If you stay with the latter, regardless of the outer conditions, you will remain in alignment with your innermost being, and through it, divine being can reach you. Spiritual practice at its no-frills simplest is a moment-by-moment learning not to do anything in a state of internal brace. Bracing is never worth the cost.[1]

It's easier to stay with safe, familiar ideas and behaviors than to risk the uncertainty of change. But in the stinging words of Austrian novelist Marie von Ebner-Eschenbach: "Old age transfigures or fossilizes."[2] The choice is ours.

Don't Believe Everything You Hear

It's hard to grow old in a culture devoted to staying young. One of the broad definitions of religion is "whatever we pay attention to." If that's true, then we've definitely made a religion of maintaining youth. What are the messages of our society that have become the accepted norm? From conversation to greeting cards, we are peppered with diminishing clichés that reflect common assumptions about aging. Though it's fun to have a chuckle about the comical parts of the process, these seemingly harmless quips shape our attitudes more than we realize. Let's put some of those current assumptions under a microscope to see how they sabotage our openness.

You Can't Teach an Old Dog New Tricks

Oh yes, you can. The students at the Meeman Center for Lifelong Learning at Rhodes College in Memphis, along with others in similar educational programs, have turned that cliché on its ear. One of my classmates at the center, a gentleman in his nineties, has explored everything from the life of Plato to life on Mars, and his insatiable curiosity keeps his brain in continuous motion. With no papers to write or exams to dread, seniors in this and other learning venues have the opportunity to unearth buried interests that were never given the time to flourish. "Old dogs" can indeed learn to weave, to speak Mandarin, to play the piano, and to peek into the fascinating world of quantum physics ... and not for the purpose of "accomplishing" something. The pure joy of learning is delicious in itself. Besides, it's invigorating to be around others who are discovering that same delight.

Age Is Just a Number

Try telling that to the arthritis in my right knee. The implication that age is merely a state of mind provokes all kinds of "yes buts." Sometimes the power of positive thinking is one more expectation that weighs me down, yet I realize the importance of optimism. There's a paradox here that must be owned. It is a "both/and" situation rather than an "either/or."

Yes, inside I'm more myself, more capable of curiosity and a surprising youthful spunk. But on the outside, there are days when the number seventy feels appallingly on target. The truth is that most of the time I want to remain sharp and stimulating, and the energy rises to fuel that desire. But there are other moments when my body wants nothing more than a hot bath to soothe aching joints right before I burrow beneath a down comforter.

It has surprised me to what degree the number seventy affects the responses of others. Many treat me differently, sometimes dismissively, like I'm in parentheses instead of part of the paragraph.

An inkling of what was to come occurred during a conversation some years ago with a young man of about twenty-five. I don't remember the face, but I remember the feeling. It was the first time I saw myself as an old lady. During our innocent exchange, his reply to me was a polite, "Yes, ma'am." It stung. Part of me knew he was exhibiting proper manners in our Southern culture; another part of me wanted to punch him. I felt as if I were being dragged across a threshold before I was ready. Surely it wasn't time for me to be considered elderly. My rebellious overreaction was quite a teaching moment. I was clearly more vulnerable to society's hidden messages than I thought.

I reluctantly recalled the scores of women throughout my young years who had received the same designation from me, for I, too, was taught to address any mature woman as "ma'am." I wondered if they had felt as insulted and categorized as I did.

Though the young man meant no disrespect (the opposite, in fact), his word touched a tender, fearful place deep inside me. Could it be that I was absorbing the ageism of our culture and pretending it wouldn't one day apply to *me*? Before I could honestly embrace the joys of later life and tackle its challenges, I obviously had to make my peace with the truth: Mother Nature would not make an exception in my case. I, too, would grow old and die. A hopeful voice inside me mused, "Surely we wouldn't have been created to live this long, if there weren't some crowning purpose in it."

My rebellious response to "ma'am" was a trigger that opened me to acceptance. Being viewed as "elderly" is difficult to accept, but it's a fact. A healthy part of aging, it seems to me, is to accept all the attendant experiences, embracing both the thirty-five-year old who still lives inside and the seventy-year-old who hauls her around.

Time Is Short

Even that one carries its own set of caveats. The seniors I interviewed gave me wildly different takes on this point of view, depending on the lens through which they were looking.

Certainly, we've all had the experience of opening birthday cards and thinking secretly, "Didn't I just celebrate a birthday a mere month ago?" The passage of days can feel like riding in a runaway car with broken brakes; we can't seem to control the speed. Yet, how do those same days feel to someone who is chronically ill or in pain or is dealing with an empty house for the first time? Loneliness and sickness can lengthen the dragging moments into an endless tick-tock that brings life to a standstill.

Even so, we can still affirm the heartfelt hope expressed in this moving benediction:

> Life is short. We don't have much time to gladden the hearts of those who travel the way with us. So be swift to love; make haste to be kind; and may the blessing of God, the Creator, and the indwelling Holy Spirit keep you now and forever.

Death Is a Disease to Be Cured

"At med school, they're teaching me that death is the *enemy*," complained a young medical student, "but sometimes it can be a friend. Why can't we look at death as a natural part of life?" His lament reflects the opinion of a growing percentage of medical professionals who are leading the charge for changes in attitudes toward death and dying. The traditional attitude has shaped the way many seniors approach their own declining health: "No matter what you have to do, or what I have to go through, just *fix* it."

The relentless search for the fountain of youth has been going on for centuries. Our fear of death shapes hospital policies, drives up health-care costs, and sends a bewildered public off to a battle it can't win. A hearty challenge to this way of thinking can direct our energies toward fashioning a good death, rather than holding the inevitable at bay. Let's work toward the day when aging will not be treated as a disease, but as a distinction.

She's Holding Up Well

When will we stop looking to the mirror as our measuring stick for wellness? No matter how enlightened we think we are, we're all prey to the failure implied by "He's past his prime," or that dreaded observation, "She's letting herself go." It flies in the face of our culture to have the courage to be who we are, sagging jowls, crow's feet, and all the rest.

In her final column before retirement, syndicated newspaper columnist Ellen Goodman had this to say:

> The phrase that kept running through my head as I considered this next step was: "I'm letting myself go." Yes ... I can see the illustration: out of shape, lazy, slovenly, the very worst things you can whisper about a woman of a certain age. But I love the idea of reclaiming that phrase. After all, where will you go when you let yourself go? To let this question fill the free space between deadlines in my life has been quite liberating. It suggests the freedom that can fuel this journey.[3]

Carol, an attractive woman of seventy-one, gave me a poignant answer to "What do you like best about growing older?" She smiled with a bit of sadness and replied, "This may sound crazy, but I love having wrinkles and being able to *own* my age. I've spent a lifetime trying to be beautiful, to dress well, to please others with my looks, because I thought it was expected of me. Thank God, I don't have to be cute anymore. I can just be *me*. If I want to wear a pretty dress and makeup, I can choose to do it, but I refuse to let my looks be the measure of my mettle."

Taking our eyes off outward appearances opens us to the possibility of aging as a process of ripening rather than rotting, as a fulfillment rather than a failure. Carol had gotten in touch with a deeper kind of beauty that doesn't diminish with age.

Leopards Can't Change Their Spots

Maybe leopards can't, but *we* can—even in our later years. The familiar assumption that change is not possible often offers us an escape hatch from healthy alterations to dysfunctional behaviors. Many hide behind the safety of "This is just the way I was reared," or the ultimate excuse, "This is the way I *am*." Not so for one seventyish woman who said that the most surprising thing she had noticed about aging was that she wasn't shackled to past patterns. She had been such a gracious "pleaser" all her life that she could hardly answer questions such as "What do *you* really think about that?" or "What restaurant would *you* like to go to?" Her "wants" had been defined by the needs of others for so long that it took months of digging and discernment to find her own inner voice. Then, of course, she had to find the courage to use that voice.

It's never too late to modify a pattern of behavior. This doesn't mean that we abandon our principles. On the contrary, healthy change often reconnects us to our deeper values that have been hijacked by modern culture.

The closer we come to life's end, the clearer these values become. One of the retirees I interviewed described the kind of attitudinal about-face required for this transition. Eugene had been a successful physician—bright, ambitious, competent, and a gifted communicator, especially with young people. His life had emphasized the familiar measures of achievement: a thriving practice, considerable wealth, and a low golf score. As he scaled back in his retirement years, he relinquished more decision-making power to the younger men in his practice. He felt not only without an identity and a full schedule, but also without meaning and purpose in his life. The initial thrill of having more time in front of the TV or on the golf course lost its luster.

Then, along came a surprise visit to the hospital emergency room. What turned out to be a treatable heart condition got his undivided attention. Some startling aha moments caused him to take a second look at his life, now more than seven decades along. He described the epiphany as a comforting clarity about his deepest values and yearnings. "I realized that though I wasn't afraid to die, I wasn't yet ready to," he quipped. "I really wanted to hang around a little longer, but I was no longer willing to fill my days with fluff. I wanted to make a real difference in the life of a real person, just like I had done in my practice."

So, armed with his natural enthusiasm and seasoned wisdom, he took his communication skills straight to a local organization for troubled boys. The God-given talents that had paved his way to success were now paving his way to meaning. His generous spirit is a gift to the young men he takes under his wing, as well as a gift to himself.

In the words of TV newsman Tom Brokaw, "It's easy to make a buck; it's tough to make a difference."[4]

It's Better to Wear Out Than to Rust Out

This piece of conventional wisdom is used to justify all kinds of behaviors. Some take it as permission to "burn the candle at both ends"; some use it constructively to kick them out of their couch-potato status. It is one of those clichés that contains a gem of truth, probably just enough to get us in trouble.

As we age, we experience a tendency to simply retire to the rocking chair and stay on the porch. Sometimes, we're weary and the inactivity just plain feels good. However, there's a difference between getting adequate rest and jeopardizing our health through laziness.

When I interviewed Doris, a woman with a number of medical issues, she revealed her own way of finding a balance between wearing out and rusting out: "I have to tend to my arthritis and my heart condition, and yes, darn it, sometimes I have to use a cane. But I just pay whatever attention my body demands, take care of it, then head out the door as fast as I can."

By the way, Doris recently graduated from college, her shock of gray hair and triumphant smile distinguishing her from the sea of young graduates. Even the local newspaper took proper notice, giving her front-page coverage. Now, at age seventy-five, she's hitting the books again, in pursuit of a master's degree.

It's All Downhill from Here

This kind of inevitability makes us feel powerless and leads to the self-fulfilling prophecy, "Just you wait; it's gonna get worse!" Though we can make a solid case for the truth of this, what about all the things that move *up*hill?

While the body declares its built-in obsolescence, the soul starts yelling, "It's *my* turn!" This interior protest reveals itself in a variety of ways—restlessness, depression, boredom, unnamed anxiety, physical symptoms, or just a vague desire for something more. It seems to be a law of nature that as the physical *de*creases, the spiritual *in*creases. However, to have an actual awareness of this increase, we must intentionally open ourselves to the spiritual growth that beckons us.

We can sabotage this natural call of the soul in a number of unconscious ways. How easily we slip into a martyr role, using phrases such as "I'll try to bear my troubles with dignity and not complain too much, because I don't want to be a burden to anyone." That may sound very gracious on the surface. In fact, we often describe such people as "growing old gracefully" when they display this demeanor of dignified resignation. But the truth is, it can cause us to miss some of the spiritual abundance that is available in our later years.

Given enough money and opportunity for diversion, we can do a bang-up job of avoiding the soul's cry for attention. We can buy a larger house, take a longer trip, get a new spouse, stave off the aging process with creams and surgery, or engage in frantic efforts to keep busy. Some of us live through our children and grandchildren, becoming "professional grandparents" rather than establishing a life of our own. These pursuits may be justified, as long as we don't use them to escape from confronting the big questions of meaning. The good is often the enemy of the best when it keeps us from attending to the spiritual health of our souls. In other words, being busy can keep us from being real. From smart phones to jet planes to Internet entertainment, abundant diversions can help us avoid stripping back the layers of our lives to discover the gold underneath.

Indeed, I believe we are hardwired by the Creator to seek meaning as we age. A number of experts on aging posit that we are fundamentally created to pursue more of a "doing" life in the first fifty years, and more of a "being" life in the years following. As we age, the pace of life may be slower, but the current runs deeper. Those who aren't afraid of this predictable progression seem to find much greater meaning in later life than those who ignore the insistent call of the soul. Why are we so afraid of this quest for meaning? In a later chapter we'll explore ways to cooperate with the spiritual hunger that gnaws at every one of us.

I'm Getting Older and Wiser

This is not necessarily true, either. Getting older is a matter of years; getting wiser is a matter of choice. In fact, Harry looked utterly puzzled when I asked him, "What have you learned about yourself as you've aged?" He finally replied that he hadn't changed at all and certainly hadn't learned anything about himself that he didn't already know. I wasn't sure whether he had misunderstood my question or I had misunderstood his answer.

It isn't always pleasant to learn the lessons of life that form us in wisdom. Experience is a tough teacher; it usually gives the test first and the lesson later. So we often take the road of least resistance, spending our time with people who affirm our prejudices and don't challenge our views—a comfortable and boring place, don't you think? A person doesn't really grow old so much as become old by not growing. In the wise words of French moralist Joseph Joubert, "The evening of a well-spent life brings its lamps with it."

Wisdom is defined as "knowledge understood, experienced, and applied." What we've understood in our heads must be experienced in our hearts and applied in our lives. To seek this kind of wisdom, we must first shed our defensiveness about our opinions and the way we've always done things and genuinely embrace openness of mind and heart. This clearly positions us in a learning stance, as voiced by none other than Socrates, who is credited with the phrase "The unexamined life is not worth living."

Changing Your Script

"Some folks are fluid and some congeal," said one observer of the aging process. We often confuse stability with rigidity. Even though we like to think of our values and opinions as the "right" ones, we should always be open to deeper understanding and to refining our positions. Unfortunately, we have a tendency to hold on to the familiar, even when it no longer serves us or when modern discoveries shoot our opinions full of holes. Even when science revealed that the Earth was round, many maintained their belief that it was flat. Even when Gus could no longer play football, he continued to push his body past its limits rather than find a new profession. Even when Cindy's kids had kids of their own, she persisted in trying to control their lives. In a similar way, later life surprises us with shifts that weren't in the script we planned. Meaningful aging requires that we rewrite our lines—not just once, but over and over.

Take a Chance

American writer Elbert Hubbard gives this advice: "The greatest mistake you can make in life is to be continually fearing you will make one."

Fear of failure is the roadblock that keeps many of us stuck in the status quo. We prefer to lose our sense of adventure rather than lose face. Taking a risk in later life is not easy and the outcome is far from certain. But there is a spurt of energy mixed with the fear when trying something new—especially when everyone tells you it's too late. It's all grist for the growth-mill anyway. God can use anything that befalls us to shape our character, whether it is wonderful or terrible, a success or a failure, or whether it is random, inflicted by another, or the result of our own stumbling. It is necessary, however, to move with the risk. In the words of Martin Luther King Jr., "Faith is taking the first step even when you don't see the whole staircase."

That gold nugget of possibility is not usually evident at first. Sometimes we have to dig like an archaeologist to find it, sifting through much emotional muck and mire to unearth the treasure. Whether the surprise brings a smile or a tear, its potential is discovered by deeply experiencing the feeling it evokes. This doesn't happen in a flash, of course. As the old saying goes, "You can't heal what you don't feel." So entering the euphoria or the despair that results from the surprising situation is part of the process.

I don't have to scroll backward very far in my own life to affirm the truth of this. At an age when my contemporaries were retiring, I discovered with alarm that it would be necessary for me to find ways to support myself financially for the rest of my life. There were a few employment opportunities for women of sixty-plus, but I felt lukewarm about the options before me. How could I possibly make a living doing what I loved to do? What I felt called to? How could I reconcile my need for security with my need to be true to myself?

My passion about the kind of work that gave me life was clear to me. After completing training in spiritual direction at the Shalem Institute and the Academy for Spiritual Formation, I was committed to bridging the gap between theology and behavior, between belief and experience. My mind was filled with finding ways of actually putting my core values into practice in ordinary life, of pursuing a harmony between words and deeds. My muddle of indecision prompted me to call a Clearness Committee, a tried-and-true Quaker practice of discernment. In brief, you gather five or six friends to prayerfully offer questions aimed at helping unearth your own deep wisdom. Within the group, there is a shared belief that God speaks through the soul. Rather than propose direct solutions, the questioners help the "focus person" hear the sacred whispers within.

It was an affirming and encouraging experience, but I felt no clarity at all as it concluded. There was a willingness to be led toward something, but I had no idea where or what. I still felt little enthusiasm for the few vocational choices that would produce the needed dollars. So I decided to wait patiently a little longer. Waiting is another thing Quakers are good at.

Some weeks later, I was blindsided by a strange phone call. "Hello, is this Linda Douty?" the caller asked. "I'm the acquisitions editor at Morehouse Publishing, and we would like to explore your writing a book for us. What are you working on now?"

My stunned reply went something like, "I'm not working on anything. (I couldn't bring myself to tell her I was emptying the dishwasher!) Who is it you were trying to reach?" As we established my identity, the strange confluence of events began to unfold. In a random romp through Internet sites by an editor in Harrisburg, Pennsylvania, a few simple entries from my teaching of a small Sunday school class on a church website had grabbed her attention. The needle-in-a-haystack occurrence was too fantastic to be ignored, even by my cynicism. I was flabbergasted.

We agreed to talk in a few days, and as I hung up the phone, my astonished excitement soon gave way to fearful demons all shouting at once. What if I fail? What if I'm too old? Because I'm not an expert on *anything*, what could I say with authority? What if I embarrassed not only myself but also my children and family? Once I calmed down, I turned to my personal litmus test for discernment, and asked myself this question: "How will I feel about this opportunity when I'm on my deathbed?"

I immediately knew the answer. Writing a book was a dream that I had buried so long ago that I had almost forgotten its existence. Even though the timing seemed rotten to me, maybe I had had to rack up sixty-four years of living to have anything worthwhile to say. Besides, in spiritual guidance sessions, I often encouraged folks toward risk taking, toward taking a leap of faith without a clear outcome. All my lofty pronouncements seemed empty if I failed to practice what I was preaching. And as for failure, even if I ended up with a little egg on my face, I would have *tried*. I would have responded to this outrageous, unpredictable, divine invitation. So I took a deep breath, dialed the editor's number, and said yes.

As it turned out, my original quest of finding financial relief didn't materialize. Though there was no windfall of money, there definitely was a windfall of meaning that made me feel incredibly alive. I've often wondered if I hadn't been in a financial strait-jacket, would I have been willing to risk failure so late in life? I doubt it.

Ronald Reagan quipped, "You know, by the time you've reached my age, you've made plenty of mistakes if you've lived your life properly."[5]

So, take a chance. If not now, when?

Be Willing to Change Your Mind

Three of the most dreaded phrases in our culture are "I'm sorry," "I've changed my mind," and "I'm not sure." Unfortunately, they're associated with the weak and lily-livered—people we think are unable to stand up for themselves or stick with a deci-sion. We label politicians as flip-floppers and judge those who compromise as unprincipled. In my view, the world would be a better place if we had more folks who were willing to change long-held opinions when they become untenable.

This is never more unsettling than when we question our religious belief systems. It takes enormous courage to dig inside, turning over the soil of our own inner landscapes. Moreover, it takes a willingness to be open to new ways of thinking, to move with the flow of life rather than against it.

Quite a number of my Christian beliefs have been chal-lenged, dissected, and reshaped during my seventy years. Though it certainly didn't seem so at the time, my faith has been strength-ened, not weakened, through the intellectual wrestling. Maybe it's because I keep returning to a scripture that is bedrock for me, "All things work together for good for those who love God" (Romans 8:28). To me, that means God can use my failures and my doubts to deepen my faith.

Being able to consider many points of view is a virtue of the strong, not the weak. The capacity to change your mind reflects humility and the intelligent pursuit of truth; those who hang on to an opinion like a dog with a bone remind me of the old cliché "My mind is made up; don't confuse me with the facts." We need constant reminders that none of us has a corner on truth.

One issue that illustrates this principle is the increasing number of folks who have changed their minds about matters of sexual orientation. The growing body of scientific evidence suggests the possibility that homosexuality is generally a matter of chromosomes, not choice. As a churchgoing woman, I grew up with the prevailing opinion that the partnership of a man and a woman was nature's way, therefore the plan ordained by God. But it only took one friendship with one gay man to change my mind.

Walter was a gifted theater director whose kindness and talent enriched the lives of those around him. In the atmosphere of the 1970s, he and his longtime partner were the butt of many unsavory jokes and much downright meanness. However, as I got to know them, I couldn't ignore their generous hearts or their moral commitment to their monogamous relationship—traits that were frequently missing in the heterosexual community. As I worked with them in the theater for several months, the situation sent me into a tailspin of confusion. My long-held convictions were squirming against the reality before me.

The tipping point came one day when Walter said sadly, "I'd give anything to be straight. Life would be so much easier." The living, breathing truth was right in front of my face: he had no choice. He was simply who he was, a suffering human being of enormous love and integrity. So, I changed my mind. Not only that, but I also committed myself to affirming the personhood and the legal rights of gays and lesbians in any way I could.

During these intervening years, I've known dozens of heterosexuals like me who have struggled with beliefs that modern science was rendering false—science that had not matured when early moral codes were shaped or sacred texts composed. I've watched friends come to grips with painful confessions of gay children and colleagues, and I continue to stand on the side of love and compassion. I can only pray that the ongoing spiritual evolution of our planet will cause us to pay attention to God's continuing revelation of truth, which invites us to change our minds.

After all, if the term "living word of God" has any validity, it must be truly alive—pulsating, shifting, and changing like the cells in a live organism.

Don't Waste Your Sorrows

Lora's simple words hinted at a much deeper reality. "I can go on," she said, "when I can see someone else who has gone on." No expert in an ivory tower has the credibility of a fellow sufferer in the trenches. Living through hardship confers an experiential PhD in Life, and those credentials call us to share what we have learned.

Poet Judy Sorum Brown reminds us that no one searches for sorrow. Yet, it visits every single one of us, invited or not.

SORROW
Sorrow's a surprise,
a sudden guest,
not seen,
quite unexpected,
appearing at my heart's door
not knocking even,
nor asking to come in,
but entering
with her own key
silently
to sit with me.[6]

Heart attacks. Suicide. Plane crashes. Loss of a child. Tragedy is an equal-opportunity visitor with no regard for race, creed, color, or social status. The sharing of pain doesn't remove the sting; it just makes it more bearable. Why? Because you can look into the eyes of someone who has been there and lived to tell it.

Marsha endured the unthinkable. After burying her first husband in 1973, she later endured the suicide of a son while caring for her terminally ill second husband. He died three months after that. The losses continued to multiply as her daughter moved seven hundred miles away and another son and daughter-in-law divorced. She found it necessary to relinquish her position as a church minister and went on a two-month sabbatical alone to bravely spend time in prayer. Though paralyzed with grief for a long time, some wise and faithful part of her knew she needed to enter God's healing process of grief with her whole heart.

She didn't shrink from the unspeakable pain. She roamed the Cape Cod beaches, threw driftwood into the surf in a rage, shook her fist at God, and experienced the anger that is a normal response to loss. She offered these reflections on those first experiences of healing: "I didn't realize it took so much energy to grieve. I was too exhausted to pray like I normally did. I rested and slept for hours on end. It felt as if I had joined the angry confusion expressed in the book of Job. There was a growing certainty that God couldn't heal what I was unwilling to feel. It hurt, but I had to be real with God if I expected God to become real for me."

Several years after that life-changing time, I asked her to pass on the wisdom she gained from that experience. She was very specific:

- Don't avoid the pain; don't cover it up with busyness.
- Get much more rest than you normally require.
- Allow others to help you; ask for what you need. (Those who want to support you feel helpless, and your honesty gives them a way to express their support. Don't make them guess what you want, even if all you want is for them to sit with you silently.)
- Lean on the traditional liturgies of the church, especially those dealing with death.
- Read the Psalms daily.
- Don't force your prayers. Allow others to pray on your behalf and claim the truth of Romans 8:26:

"Likewise the Spirit helps us in our weakness, for we do
not know how to pray as we ought, but that very Spirit
intercedes with sighs too deep for words."

Marsha eventually poured her energy and experience into
action, founding a ministry for survivors of suicide, traveling
far and wide with her message of hope and healing. She is also
a gifted spiritual director with a special interest in bereavement
counseling. She didn't waste her sorrows; she allowed God to
use them to bring comfort and wisdom to the lives of others. In
that process, she found surprising meaning in her own life.

Henry was a prominent retired professor of psychology
who had wrestled for years with the chronic pain of neuropathy,
then with cancer. Through doggedly discovering ways to
manage his own pain, he was led to organize a support group
for others suffering from the same condition. They exchanged
medical information, swapped stories of their lives, and supported each other with strong bonds of friendship.

The challenge is this: be willing to offer your own experience of sorrow to God for the healing of others, and just watch
what happens. People who need your hand of comfort and credibility will drift into your life. No matter how many helping
hands are extended to hurting folks, the hand they will grasp is
the one that has been there—hurting in the same ways, surviving in the same ways, and sharing that experience with grace
and generosity.

Accept the Mystery of the Unplanned

On a recent trip to a bookstore, I noticed the abundance of titles
teasing us toward certainty with phrases such as "Finding God's Plan
for You," "Discovering Your Purpose in Life," and "How to Know the
Will of God." Not only are such words misleading, but they divert
us from the benefits of befriending the uncertainties in life.

Teresa's life had unfolded pretty much on schedule—a loving
husband, three thriving children, even two sets of grandparents still
alive and active in their eighties. With their history of remarkable

health and love of travel, she and her husband were looking forward to the coziness and freedom of the empty nest.

Then, the pathway took a surprising turn. After a debilitating accident, their daughter returned home to live permanently with them. Their own parents began to decline—all four at the same time—and the other two children experienced the pain and problems of divorce. Teresa and Ted watched the exciting life they had planned begin to slip from their grasp. The carefree hours they had anticipated were filled with visits to hospitals and doctors, spontaneous babysitting for grandchildren, and providing financial rescue for their struggling adult children. Because they made a conscious decision to shift gears and let go of their own expectations, they became flourishing members of the "sandwich generation." Adapting to the unplanned flow of life, they decided who they were going to *be* rather than what they were going to *do*.

Unless we take our hands off the wheel and allow Spirit to lead the way, later life can become an endless line of frustrations. Adjusting to what is puts us in the flow of life. Besides, most of our projected agendas are ultimately shattered anyway.

So keep your eyes alert and your heart open and take the leap of radical trust. You won't be sent a detailed template of your future, but you can notice opportunities, discover your gifts, uncover deep interests, and become more aware of how *who* you are can meet the needs of *where* you are. Author and spiritual leader David Steindl-Rast reminds us that "life-giving water [is available], if you will only open your heart and drink."[7]

Make Music with What You Have

"I hate to say this, but Mother has become tiresome and boring, and we all dread being around her," said my young friend Carla. "We totally understand her situation, but she won't stop talking about it. Her health is declining and she's unable to help with the meals and grandchildren when we have family get-togethers, and the family accepts that. I just wish *she* could accept it ... we're tired of hearing her apologize."

Carla's mom wasn't being avoided because she was no longer "useful" but because her constant complaints made the atmosphere around her toxic and depressing. "I *would* be helping if I only could," she whined. "I just feel terrible about being such a burden." Carla ended our lunch conversation with an insightful remark. "I wish she would concentrate on what she *can* do," she lamented, "rather than what she *can't*."

Simple enough, right? Yet Mom continued to sabotage her own cheerfulness and those in her relational orbit by dwelling on her limitations. What Carla needed was her mother's honest offer of reading to the children, rocking the baby, telling childhood stories to the older ones, or giving kitchen instructions for her famous mashed potatoes. The family valued her presence, not her protests.

Later life demands a fluidity that allows us to constantly shift gears, adapt to the changes, and focus on what we can still do. A heartwarming illustration of this principle is the true story of a performance by the renowned violinist Itzhak Perlman. From listening to him play, you might not know that Perlman suffered from polio as a child. To this day he walks slowly and deliberately across the stage with the help of two crutches and heavy braces on his legs. His patient listeners always know that it takes him several minutes to put down the crutches, unclasp the braces, and place the violin under his chin.

During one performance at Lincoln Center, the unthinkable happened: one of his violin strings snapped in mid-performance, and everything stopped. His audience anticipated a long delay while he reattached his braces and exited to correct the problem. But they were in for a surprise. He waited a moment, then signaled the conductor to continue where they had left off. After he completed the symphonic work *with only three strings*, playing with incomparable passion and determination, the people came to their feet in appreciative applause. Perlman coaxed them to quiet and responded with a soft smile, "You know, sometimes it is the artist's task to find out how much music you can still make with what you have left."[8]

What a powerful line that is. And who knows—perhaps that is *the way* of life, not just for artists, but for all of us. Perhaps our task in this shaky, fast-changing, bewildering world is to make music, at first with all that we have, and then, when that is no longer possible, to make music with what we have left.

The obvious point is this: whether the surprise comes in the form of calamity or a stroke of luck (or a mixture of both), a door of possibility is presented. On the other side of that door is something new, whether it's a fresh project, a fresh thought, or a fresh approach to the future. It takes considerable courage to walk through that door with no guarantees—except that the Presence that beckons you forward is the same Presence that greets you on the other side.

There's a tendency to consider later life as a time to get our affairs in order to prepare for the Grand Exit, to wrap up the loose ends. As it turns out, that's a minor detail. If we're open to it, we will be surprised by the invitation to explore the spiritual significance of everything we are and all that we do. Years ago, French philosopher and Jesuit theologian Pierre Teilhard de Chardin observed that "we are not human beings having a spiritual experience. We are spiritual beings having a human experience."[9] One of the spiritual surprises of this stage is the opportunity to more deeply understand that reality.

We began this chapter with the recognition of two doors—one leading to resistance and stagnation and the other leading to growth and expansion. If you feel ready to walk through that second challenging door, remember that openness is the key that turns the lock.

Looking Inside

1. Among the attributes listed in the "resistance group" and the "growth group," which ones seem to describe your current feelings and attitudes?

2. Do you think people are capable of real change? Why or why not? Cite life examples that you have observed in each category.

3. Examine your natural thoughts about death. Where do you see traces of fear and traces of faith?

4. Name one thing that has repeatedly piqued your curiosity, but that you've been unable or unwilling to pursue. How might you honor that impulse?

5. What words or attitudes or habits would you need to let go of to move more freely toward growth in later life?

2

Surprises of the Self

Just be yourself. Everyone else is taken.
OSCAR WILDE

So, what has surprised you about aging?" I inquired. "Is there something that no one told you about?"

Shirley paused thoughtfully before replying, "No one told me that I would finally be comfortable in my own skin. You might say that I'm more *myself* now than I've ever been in my life. And it feels really good."

Harold answered a bit differently. "I had no idea that these years would be as fulfilling as they are. There's this surprising freedom—even with my heart condition. I've let go of my need to compete, to be right, to *win*. And I've discovered another part of me that I didn't know was there."

"Could you describe that 'part'?" I pressed.

"The part that slows down and listens, the part that searches for meaning—the *mystical* part, I guess." Then he added, "I've always been considered an extrovert, an outgoing, talkative guy. I hadn't noticed that there was an introverted part of me hiding inside."

Poet and philosopher Mark Nepo views that "part" in spiritual terms: "Each person is born with an unencumbered spot—free of expectation and regret, free of ambition and embarrassment, free of fear and worry—an umbilical spot of grace where we were each first touched by God."[1]

This "part" has been called by many names, and maybe the words depend on the lens you are looking through or the language that carries meaning for you. For instance, psychologists refer to the psyche; Jung called it the Authentic Self; Hindu masters call it Atman; Buddhists call it Dharma; Sufis call it Qalb; theologians often call it soul; Jesus regarded it as the "heart" of us, the center where Love is born.

In the wise words of Pastor Steve Garnaas-Holmes,

> The true self is not something we can create; it is a gift. To pay attention to the present moment and to attend to *What Is* in us and to choose to be our God-given selves … is an interior experience of the Realm of Grace, the "Kingdom of God." The more we practice this presence, the more fully we can resist the world's anxieties and its fear-based divisions, and proclaim the Realm of God. When we are faithful to our true selves in God, we participate in the healing of the world.[2]

Later life is a time when many of us get off the treadmill and turn our attention to connecting with this timeless spot of grace where God whispers in our souls and shows us who we really are. Moving from an adaptive self to a true self is not so much a metamorphosis as a growing clarity, an acquaintance with our essence. The process is a bit like applying window cleaner to a murky windowpane and wiping, wiping, wiping until the clarity is revealed.

Because our culture has a tendency to reward achievement and extroversion, our own need for reflection can go unmet for decades, leaving our interior landscape barren and uncultivated. The elders I interviewed had plenty to say about what they found, once they had the courage to travel that inner safari. They discovered all manner of buried treasures, buried fears, and buried dreams.

Ann's experience of this inner journey, however, was frightening rather than exhilarating. A musician since the age of nine, she had been shaped by the world of keyboards and melodies. Whether she was performing or teaching, music had formed and filled her identity—much more than she realized. In her sixties, when arthritis crept into her hands and stifled her skills at the piano, she felt invisible, not only as a musician but as a *person*.

"I was terrified," she explained. "It was as if I knocked on the door of my own heart and there was nobody home. Without music to define me, I had no idea who I was." Ann was faced with the task of discovering herself apart from that lifelong role. It was far from easy.

Hearing the call of the soul takes time—it can't be rushed. It rarely works if we scurry to solutions. Instead, we can stay with the confusion rather than try to fix it, allowing ourselves not to feel "at the top of our game" during such a search. We must lean with confidence and courage into the uncertainty it brings. When the classic roles of the first half of life desert us, a mixture of anxiety and adventure is sure to lurk around.

"When I retired," confided Clifford, "I felt rootless, untethered, floating, diminished. It took a while to discover how much ego investment I had in my work." Responses such as those of Clifford and Ann seemed to have little gender basis. Women and men both described the same kind of emotional vacuum at this time of life, though they expressed it differently. Whether invested as wife or mother, mechanic or CEO, from the boardroom to the bedroom, the challenge of change was temporarily unsettling.

In *Finding Meaning in the Second Half of Life*, author and Jungian analyst James Hollis writes:

> In most cases we come to this point in our life serving a diminished view of ourselves. As Jung once put it humorously, we all walk in shoes too small for us.... We engage our soul's agenda, which requires a humbled attitude and a wary watchfulness. It requires that we understand that our lives,

even when fraught with outer difficulties, are always unfolding from within.[3]

If we approach later life only as a time when we get to choose what we *do*, we've missed half the richness. It's also a time when we can find out who we *are*.

I'm Still Me!

Gina is eighty-six and proud of it. As we sipped a cup of tea in her retirement apartment, she clearly relished the opportunity to review her fascinating life. When the subject of surprise came up, however, she said without hesitation, "Oh, honey, the biggest surprise is that I'm still *me!*"

She wasn't the only person who responded this way. I began to wonder what the sense of "me" was that seems to follow us from stage to stage and year to year. While we're growing more wrinkled and wise, there is an ageless core of us with an original imprint—the real *me*. Life lessons may be learned and opinions may change, but there's a self that travels with us from one city to another, one marriage to another, one circumstance to another. It moves with us in a solitary dance, unaffected by the ravages of time, yet altered and clarified by our life experiences.

Moreover, sometimes the "me" seems to get lost in the shuffle. Our younger years of earning and spending, reacting and responding to the expectations of others, slowly form a film over that essence. Barnacles, maybe. In any case, that core gets layered over by life.

Then along come the later years, a time for wiping away the film, peeling back the layers, chipping off the barnacles, sweeping away the things that don't belong. As we peel back the decades, the gifts of aging can be revealed. It's time to become friends with that neglected authentic self.

What Is Me and What Isn't

Ron, a "doer" by nature, had this to say: "I no longer have anything to prove. All that serial activity is not necessary anymore; I don't have to operate at full throttle. In fact, I'm not running on that competitive track ever again; that's not who I am now." However, there were attributes Ron wanted to hang on to—his adventurous streak, his curiosity, his capacity for productivity. He wanted to bring them with him into a different arena—reclaiming his contemplative nature, his quieter self, along with discovering the wonder of sitting still.

A product of traditional women's roles, Stella wanted to say goodbye to what she called her "Cinderella self." She wanted to develop her own independence rather than wait for another Prince Charming to produce a glass slipper that would fit. Her knee-jerk instinct had usually been something like "Tell me what to be, and I'll be it." She had tried to shape herself into whatever she thought the man in her life wanted.

But then she did the work of searching for who she was underneath all that adaptive behavior. Her final words to me were said somewhat sheepishly: "You know what I found out? I discovered that I'm smart. I don't need someone to take care of me. Goodness, I'm even competent!" She had been marching to someone else's tune for so long that it took time to sing her own song.

It seems harder to sustain a false persona as we age. A need bubbles up from some sacred place within us to retain and expand the authentic parts of ourselves, and let the rest go. So how do we sort this out? What parts of our personas do we need to let go and what parts do we want to take with us into later life?

We toss around the encouraging cliché, "Just be *yourself*" as if it were a light switch we could flip on. Finding ourselves takes patience, intention, and watchfulness. Then we have the opportunity to shed the parts that don't really fit our true selves, parts that evolved as a sort of window dressing for public viewing. However, beware of labeling these parts of ourselves as "good" or "bad." Rather than engage in self-condemnation, such as, "I was so *stupid* to make that choice," remember that nothing is wasted in God's divine economy. Our failures and strong points, our successes and weaknesses—all are grist for the growth mill.

Though we yearn to connect with this core inside us, the insightful writer Parker Palmer reminds us that it's a tricky business, comparing the soul's shy nature to that of an animal in the wild.

> Like a wild animal, the soul is tough … it knows how to survive in hard places…. Yet despite its toughness, the soul is also shy…. If we want to see a wild animal, we know that the last thing we should do is go crashing through the woods, yelling for it to come out. But if we will walk quietly into the woods, sit patiently at the base of a tree … the creature we seek might put in an appearance.[4]

If we're serious about wanting the soul to speak, we must develop the listening skills that will allow us to hear it. As we become more familiar with that unique voice through which God reveals our essence, we find vital information about ourselves: our natural wiring, our talents, our preferences. In addition, we learn to distinguish between what we're supposed to feel and what we really do feel.

A beginning point is being sensitive to the things that signal aliveness. What causes you to break into a smile? When are you moved to tears? When do you lose track of time? When do you feel an unexpected "oomph"? A spurt of energy? A sense of calm and peace? Write that information down in detail, noting the circumstances. Were you alone or with others? Which friends shared or supported that experience? All these feelings are part of everyday life, but most of us ignore them as they send their vital messages.

Conversely, begin to notice the things that bring you down. When do you feel enveloped by a dark cloud, bored silly, dulled, or deadened? Catalog those circumstances as well.

An important caveat here: be careful not to confuse dullness with sadness. Genuine grief and heartbreaking sadness are as much a part of being alive as are joy and jubilation. The soul-stealing experiences are those infused with bleak feelings of emptiness.

This condition goes by many names: ennui, lethargy, boredom, torpor, the "blahs." Noted writer Kathleen Norris uses the ancient term coined by monks centuries ago: *acedia*. She writes:

> *Acedia* may be an unfamiliar term to those not well versed in monastic history or medieval literature. But that does not mean it has no relevance for contemporary readers.... Languages have a life and a wisdom of their own, and the reemergence of the word suggests to me that acedia is the lexicon's version of a mole, working on us while hidden from view.... [W]hile we may find it convenient to regard it as a more primitive word for what we now term depression, the truth is much more complex.... I think it likely that much of the restless boredom, frantic escapism, commitment phobia, and enervating despair that plagues us today is the ancient demon of acedia in modern dress.... I would suggest that while depression is an illness treatable by counseling and medication, acedia ... is best countered by spiritual practice and the discipline of prayer.[5]

In an interview following the publication of her book *Acedia & Me*, she defined acedia as the spiritual aspect of sloth—that is, not caring, or being unable to care, and ultimately being unable to care that you don't care. She further referred to the condition as spiritual morphine, masking not only pain but also causing a loss of faith in ourselves and in our relationship with God. In a secular culture, we often subsume our spiritual needs under psychological symptoms and treatments and find ourselves disappointed when those resources don't mend our wounded souls.

Yet another probing set of questions about your authentic self centers around childhood memories. What did you instinctively do as a child when left to your own devices? What were your natural inclinations when freed from parental influence or suggestion?

Purchase a journal precisely for the purpose of this interior quest. Start writing down your honest reactions—free of *ought tos* and *shoulds*—and do it every single day. Remember you're not talking about someone else's preferences, or what you wish you felt, but those uncluttered responses of your own soul. These come from that hallowed home inside where the spirit of God shows you how you were created. Over the space of a few weeks, you'll see patterns emerge, things as simple as the joy of seeing a yellow finch at the feeder, or as complex as a desire to build a Habitat for Humanity house. Wake up to the sorts of things the Spirit is showing you about your own wiring, your own gifts.

Getting to know this emerging self is not always pretty. As we begin to notice the things that delight us or dull us, we will also become aware of things about ourselves that are harmful to us and to others. My two sons have been my most straightforward critics through the years, and I have probably neglected to thank them—not only for the affirmation they have provided, but also for the lessons that cut me off at the knees. First as youngsters and now as adult men, they seem to see my "stuff" much more consciously and clearly than I do, and they don't hesitate to tell me about it. In one of my previous books I described one of their revealing confrontations:

> The time was early evening, that familiar family rush hour when everything converges at 5 o'clock—dinner preparation, homework, and the race against time for a variety of 7 o'clock meetings. As I dashed around the kitchen (efficiency-mode in high gear), slamming cabinet doors and calling out instructions, Harrison gently elbowed David and said knowingly, "She's doing it again."
>
> Barely overhearing his stage whisper, I demanded to know what he meant.... Finally, Harrison explained with a sigh, "Mom, every time you have too much on your plate and get into such a snit, you have a way of poisoning the atmosphere around here!"
>
> My angry reaction was suddenly blunted by an inner awareness that I needed to pay attention. Suppressing my

defensiveness, I said, "I don't know what you mean. Explain this to me." And to my dismay, they did.

They pantomimed my jerky body language, mimicked the tone of my voice, portraying the picture of a duty-driven woman whose anxiety and resentment were contagious.... I said, "I don't want to be this way ... please help me change this."

The boys explained that they could see it coming long before it erupted. They could sense the buildup.... It had become such a familiar persona that I was unable to see it coming. After much discussion, we arrived at a plan, one that would preclude any verbal confrontation. When either of them sensed the hectic pattern on the horizon, he would gently hold up a "stop" hand in front of my face, alerting me to the situation with no words spoken by either of us.

During the weeks that followed, I was humbled by the degree to which I was unconscious of my behavior. Time after time, I was surprised by a hand rising in front of my face, and I slowly made progress toward awareness. I could let go of this toxic mask only as I faced it honestly and willingly.[6]

Anytime we have a genuine desire to know ourselves better, we receive the whole package—the things that please us and the things that dismay us. Anything unlived or unrecognized is lurking in the shadow. Some of those tendencies and traits are happy discoveries that we welcome into the light of consciousness. Some are hidden motivations that may not make us proud. Unfortunately, the shadow sides of even our "good" traits are not usually a secret to others. No matter how positive an attribute may appear to be, when taken to the extreme, a negative side becomes evident.

- The gift of efficiency, if exercised over the top and without sensitivity, can diminish the efforts of others.

Moreover, as my sons can attest, it creates a toxic and anxious atmosphere.

- The virtue of goodness can easily drift into spiritual pride (a condition that most faith traditions warn us about).
- Wisdom can become patronizing, infused with an air of superiority.
- Beauty can become vanity.
- Love can become infiltrated with jealousy and possessiveness.
- Loyalty can be a mask for blind trust.
- Tolerance can turn into indifference.
- Self-confidence can easily become arrogance.
- Faith can be tinged with self-righteousness.

To become intimately acquainted with yourself is not a search for flaws; it is an honest awareness of the flaws along with the treasures. Only by owning this messy mixture of the true self's wholeness can a thoughtful person make wise choices. Because we can't let go of what we can't see, the first step is always a long, hard look at ourselves. As we unearth those things that are sabotaging our growth and name them, then the hard work of letting go of them is before us. Often we transfer that burden to God, praying that God will "take it from us" with little effort on our part. I wish it were that easy. *God will not take away that which we refuse to release*—no matter how fervently we pray for it. For instance, we may pray "Lord, please make me less judgmental" without monitoring our own judgmental words and the critical thoughts that cause them. What we persistently give our attention to grows.

Writer Steve Garnaas-Holmes described yet another way to uncover these hidden motivations:

In this 500-channel, multisensory, hyperactive world, what do you give your attention to? Do you follow your favorite team? Watch the weather? Track the stock market? Keep tabs on movie stars?...

Do you fasten your attention on fear and anxiety, or do you keep your eyes peeled for grace? Is your radar tuned to people's judgments, or do you attend to the love of God within you? Do you fill your consciousness with past mistakes, fears of the future, things you regret or dread or the way you wish things were—especially the way you wish things were—or do you pay attention to the present moment?

What do you see? What is true in you and around you right now? What is happening this moment? How is your breathing? Start there. Stay there. Don't distract yourself with stuff you don't need to fret about. Pay attention to the present moment, without analyzing, assuming, wishing or correcting. It's not that you shouldn't hope, or treasure a vision for yourself and the world. It's just that you begin with the present moment, without judgment or preconception. Rather than trying to manipulate your reality into what you want, be available to the grace that is hidden in what is. Simply be present. You'll be surprised how lovely it is.[7]

In the words of Hawaiian shaman Serge Kahili King, "Energy flows where attention goes."[8] That may seem like a trite bumper sticker, but it's true.

Your Orphaned Creative Child

Steve was eighty-two when he picked up his first palette and paintbrush. He had spent his life sorting numbers instead of colors, and retirement allowed him to return to his first love—the sea. Leisurely hours on a sailboat introduced him to more shades of blue than he thought existed. The colors led him to a canvas, then a seaside scene, then another and another. Soon he connected with a hidden artist inside him who had been patiently waiting in the wings for decades.

Before you say "But I can't paint!" and turn to the next chapter, let's look at this matter of creativity through a wider lens. Remember that part of Genesis that tells us we were made "in the image of God"? Surely the Great Creator placed a creative spark, a seed of possibility, within each one of us. The flourishing and flowering of that seed is an expression of our true nature. Unfortunately for many of us, that creative child within has not been parented well. We haven't nurtured that spark or watered the seed, or rocked that neglected child. Instead, we've allowed it to be diminished, banished to a corner, devalued, and, yes, orphaned.

To recover that neglected part of ourselves, we don't need to paint the *Mona Lisa* or write *War and Peace*. We merely need to live creatively. What if we found artistic solutions to situations in front of our eyes—a new way to arrange the tools in the garage or cook a great pot of soup? In planning an exciting activity for the grandchildren, trace the threads of memory back to your own childhood for inspiration. Recall those original impulses and pleasures, and give fresh expression to them.

Kimberly was intentional about connecting to her creative child. When she retired from a successful career in retail marketing, there were months of disorientation and finally an evaluation of the years ahead of her. Then she enrolled in a course called "The Artist's Way," which encouraged her to listen to the voices inside her and follow their lead. The eye for beauty and the talent for reproducing it that made her a valued part of her company were still present. It was part of a creative reservoir of energy inside her that was much deeper than she realized. And that energy wanted another outlet.

The more she gave wings to her creativity, the more it soared. She had to let go of its destination and flight pattern and where it wanted to land. She engaged in fearless trial and error— weaving, felting, dyeing, collaging, scrapbooking, bookmaking, knitting, and just about anything related to fiber arts.

One day she realized that this energy had been there as far back as she could remember, urging her to bring order out of chaos, tease beauty out of banality. As a young minister's wife, she had transformed many a somber parsonage into a delightful dwelling for her family. Later, after extensive schooling at the New York Institute of Design, she moved into the business world. The capacity to see possibilities for harmony and richness, then turn them into realities, had always been a natural part of her life. She simply hadn't seen that seed as creativity. The more she watered it, the more it blossomed. Instead of using that talent to make a living, she began using it to make a life.

Marsha is what most would call a left-brain person—intelligent, direct, pragmatic, decisive, organized, and very precise. When I asked her about her greatest surprise in later life, she replied without hesitation, "I discovered that, of all people, I have a creative streak." Mere curiosity carried her into a class for adult beginning painters, but she didn't stop there. Soon she converted an upstairs bedroom into an artist's retreat, where she loses herself in shapes and colors.

When I asked what advice she would like to pass along to other seniors, her energetic response was quick: "Tell folks to find their creative impulse—turns out everyone has it. Then own it, honor it, and find a way to live it out." Marsha's religious faith led her to express this creative energy in service to the community. She works weekly with underprivileged children in the "Music for Esteem" project at her church and, despite a number of physical setbacks, is a clear example of thriving, rather than surviving. The ongoing consequences of an early automobile accident took her through the throes of a knee replacement (she replaced her walking exercises with swimming), a chronic ankle malfunction (surgery again), and a lingering limp (which she just puts up with). Yet, she consistently finds ways to be of service to her community.

Like Marsha, James was brainy. His soaring intellect had brought him considerable success as a psychiatrist. He had spent his life diagnosing, unraveling, and treating serious cases of mental illness. As he moved closer to retirement, it was as if his heart began tugging and his hands began "itching." Soon he found himself at a potter's wheel having the time of his life. Though he didn't produce any masterpieces, he met his own creative, neglected inner child, and they had a terrific time together.

But it isn't all about developing a skill with your hands. Edith, a woman I met almost twenty years ago, introduced me to a much broader concept of creativity. When the two of us were neighbors in a Dallas suburb, Edith taught me some secrets about living creatively that still guide me today, especially at this life juncture. As the wife of a successful corporate executive, she was subject to frequent relocations to cities around the country. In fact, she had hauled the three children and all their belongings from place to place every two years or so.

As our new friendship grew, I asked her one day how she did it, how she managed to thrive in what seemed to me an impossible situation. I'll never forget her thoughtful reply: "I try to look at it this way ... every couple of years, I get an opportunity to redefine my life and the life of our family. I take a look at what worked for us in this particular location, and in a way 'pack it up' and take it with us. I get clear about what lessons we learned, individually and as a family. What kinds of friends seemed to bring out the best in us? What part of our lives here reflected our true values? We take those parts with us and leave the rest behind." Her life was an example of creativity in action.

As you can see, some folks found something totally new and different in their creative well. Some took traits they had honed in their vocational lives and shaped them in another direction. Some learned to live the life they were already living in a more imaginative way. But they all had one thing in common: they stopped giving excuses as to why they couldn't write or paint or imagine or play the guitar or take a chance on being less than perfect. They stopped saying, "Yes, but..." You can finish that sentence in any number of ways.

- Yes, but I'm not talented.
- Yes, but I don't have time.
- Yes, but I'll make a fool of myself.
- Yes, but he won't let me.
- Yes, but she needs me.
- Yes, but they won't be my friends anymore.
- Yes, but it's too much work.

I suppose we would all like to have a glorious garden that someone else tends. Then we could simply gather the flowers without expending any effort. Unfortunately, this is not the case in our interior gardens. We must till that creative soil ourselves, keeping it rich and receptive to continued divine planting, and then water it like the dickens.

Sometimes the pattern of pretending becomes so automatic that we lose touch with what we actually want. Maybe that's why I celebrate the honesty that later life invites.

The Vanishing Social Filter

For all my talk of harmony and congruence within the self, I must assert that we're still a bundle of contradictions. Acceptance of our own inconsistencies is necessary for sanity and humility.

Claire conveyed some fascinating insights when she answered the question "What have you discovered about yourself during this stage of life?" Her comments introduced me to the concept of the social filter through which most of our words and actions pass.

"I was taught to please those around me, to make them comfortable, to say the right thing at the right time, to project the image of a *nice person*," she explained. "In my day, we were taught to get what we wanted through charm, not directness. Everything passed through an unconscious test that became second nature: What should I say? What will they think? How can I keep all these balls in the air and keep everyone happy at the same time? Well, at age seventy-five, I'm sick of doing that. My social filter is worn out from overuse!" She had no desire to lose her sense of kindness or appropriateness, but she longed to temper those traits with a healthy dose of honesty.

Oddly enough, the more you connect with your true self and stop trying to be something you're not, the more likely you are to feel like a misfit now and then. It's an enormous comfort to me that the Bible is full of examples of flawed folks who were loved and valued and used by God. What a relief. Joseph was a master manipulator; Moses was a poor speaker and tried to wiggle out of his assignment; David had the husband of his paramour killed. Yet all made contributions to humankind, even with their glaring shortcomings.

Those who shared their opinions and stories with me gave many self-described examples of feeling out of sync with the norms around them. Sharon confided, "I have deep religious faith and spiritual convictions. I love silent retreats, but I also enjoy an occasional dry martini made with really good gin. That combination makes me feel too spiritual for the martini crowd and too worldly for the church crowd. Thank goodness, I've found some other misfits to hang around with!" Then she added this quip: "A jigger of gin is probably not as harmful as the plate full of fat-laden casseroles eaten at many church suppers, but I won't argue that point. I may be a bundle of contradictions, but at age seventy-one, it feels good to say who I am, warts and all."

There were a significant number of respondents who felt they didn't totally fit with the denominations or faith groups in which they participated. Burt said it this way: "The Christian container seems too tight; the Buddhist container feels too loose. If I go to the Unitarian church, I miss the familiar Christian liturgy. If I visit a Quaker meeting, I miss the music. Now I no longer try to fit with everyone else's way of worship. It's more authentic for me to live into more important questions, such as: 'Who or what is God to me?' or 'How can I truly love my neighbor as myself?' The older I get, the more comfortable I am with saying that I don't know, or that I'm still working on that."

Let's shift that feeling from the religious arena to the social scene. Sometimes we get in touch with the real "me" hiding under the adaptive "me" through trivial circumstances. I learned part of this lesson on the golf course.

I've never been particularly athletic, nor have I actually enjoyed competitive sports. But I've tried—oh, how I've tried. After years of golf clinics and tournaments and acquiring a closet full of golf gear, I had a memorable moment when I finally leveled with myself about my relationship with the game. I had spent years trying to be something I wasn't, attempting to fit into a social golf world that held little meaning for me. I appreciated the design of a good golf course, laid out with beauty and precision. I loved the (occasional) harmony in my body when I managed to swat the ball down the fairway. But the idea of knocking a white ball toward a tiny hole in the ground and keeping track of the knocks was never the point for me. Most of the time, I forgot to count the shots or even to write the number on the score card. I recalled and recorded those feelings during a writing-class exercise titled "What If It Hadn't Rained?" When our teacher assigned that topic, my mind returned to that revealing moment.

> If it hadn't rained, I might not have realized the bare truth of what I was doing ... the truth without all the rationalizations and justifications. I would have hurriedly grabbed my golf clubs, stuck a package of peanut butter crackers in with my new golf glove, and headed for the club. I would have taken out my trusty three-wood and stuck a tee in the ground, nervously hoping for a decent drive on the long par five. But the thunderstorm mercifully struck, and I knew the tournament would be postponed.
>
> Suddenly I was overwhelmed with an emotion that surprised and startled me. Its name was RELIEF.
>
> Relief that I didn't have to perform.
>
> Relief that I didn't have to spend the entire day coaxing that ball toward the hole.

Relief that I didn't have to make mindless small talk about pars and birdies for five hours.

Relief that I didn't have to compete for something not worth winning.

Relief that I didn't have to pretend I was having fun.

Why hadn't I recognized the pretense? Why was I doing this? It was a familiar pattern. I was caught again in a web of expectations that I automatically adopted as my own.

Sure, there were times when I relished the aroma of freshly mown grass, the feel of my body in a synchronized swing, the sharp crack of the club hitting the sweet spot. But the truth was that by the eighth hole, I was wishing it were the eighteenth.

So I secretly welcomed the rain. It was the agent of my liberation, the spark that ignited my awareness of who I was or ... wasn't. "Face it," I said to myself, "You are NOT a real golfer. You're just a person whose favorite color happens to be green."

I poured myself another cup of coffee and watched the glistening drops splash steadily against the windowpane. Sighing, I pulled the afghan up over my lap, daring to ask myself a brand-new question: "What do you really WANT to do with this unexpected gift of a day?" After a slight pause, I reached for the thick book, untouched on the nightstand, and with a smile, I turned to page one.[9]

A glimpse of the true self can happen anytime, anyplace, anywhere. The process of seeing ourselves clearly is like getting into a glass-bottomed boat where you watch all the deep-sea creatures lurking beneath the surface—resentment sharks, stingrays of greed, colorful swimmers, camouflaged creatures. It amounts to observing the laboratory of your mind, collecting data, and then taking appropriate action. As you gain a little detachment from your emotional patterns, you can stand back when the mind is agitated and see how often it makes mountains out of molehills.

Which leads me to another layer of self-awareness—that of taking responsibility for our ego stuff. It's been said that one mark of a spiritually mature person is the growing capacity *not* to take things personally. Marsha offered this insight: "Any time I get my feelings hurt, it's a blinking red light that my ego is needy and wants to be in control. I'm allowing the opinions and behavior of others to determine my moods or reactions, and most of the time, it has nothing to do with *me*. People have their own filter through which they see things, as well as their own problems. I'm at the place in my life now where I don't need others to make me happy—even my own children. I may *want* them to approve of me, but I don't *need* them to. It's liberating for me and for them."

Buried Dreams

How would you complete the sentence "I've always wanted to … "?

When I posed the question "What would you like to experience before you die?" the respondents gave me an astounding array of unfulfilled dreams. They ran the gamut from traveling to the Alps to writing an autobiography, from learning to speak French to learning to love, from cleaning out the attic to cleaning up a cluttered schedule.

There were a significant number of frustrated writers. Margaret wanted to complete a family history to hand down to grandchildren. Joe wanted to publish a collection of poems. Ross was haunted by an urge to share his experiences of caring for a wife with Alzheimer's. A children's book, a mystery novel, a cookbook—many dreams of finally putting pen to paper had been abandoned on the altar of procrastination and fear of failure.

I can attest to this: the only way to get a book written is to *start*. You don't have to write the whole thing. Just follow the form for a brief book proposal. Write a table of contents. Label a folder ("The Book") and start filling it with ideas, words, images. Join a writer's group where fledgling authors encourage one another. Besides, other writers won't let you get away with not writing.

In general, many in later life experienced a waning of their wanderlust. They had little enthusiasm and energy to spend on travel for travel's sake. A majority were interested only in trips that were meaningful in some way, those that focused on the inner journey as well as the outer journey. Sally wanted to go to Machu Picchu while she was still in hiking form; Mel longed to spend a week at a monastery to deepen his relationship with God; Ray simply dreamed of circling a redwood tree, standing on a glacier, watching a whale. Quite a few respondents were interested in pilgrimages to sacred sites, such as the Scottish island of Iona, the pyramids at Giza, or Stonehenge. One yearned to follow in the footsteps of St. Paul to Corinth. All were eager to experience something significant in their souls, not just get another stamp on their passports.

But what about the travel dreams that can't be realized at this late date? Rather than contaminate the desire with disappointment and regret, here are a few suggestions from the seniors I interviewed:

- Check out a travel video or *National Geographic* photo shoot of the location.
- Talk to those who've been there; ask to see their albums and travel diaries.
- Ask them how it felt to be there. What were the best and worst moments of the trip?
- Google the location on the Internet and print out information.
- Check out or purchase colorful travel books focusing on the location and imagine yourself in the middle of the scenes that are depicted.

I followed their suggestions as I let go of a long-held travel dream, and it helped. For many years, I have longed to experience the grandeur of the fjords of Norway from the ocean, then follow the Baltic Sea around to the Hermitage in St. Petersburg. There I would sit before Rembrandt's eight-foot painting *Return of the*

Prodigal Son all day long, just as Henri Nouwen described in his moving book by the same name. As the chances grow slim that I'll ever physically get there, I bought the video *The Song of Norway* and watched it several times. Now I'm rereading Nouwen's *Return of the Prodigal Son*, experiencing the Rembrandt painting through his sensitive spirit and powerful words. In a way, I feel as if I've been there. Sometimes if we can't take a journey physically, we can take it vicariously.

A more intentional spiritual life was a theme that ran through quite a number of dreams. Gerald wanted to spend the next years using his organizational skills to help struggling churches survive and strengthen. Lola vowed to spend more time "basking in the light of God" so that she could reflect that light to every person she encountered. Donald was dedicating himself to becoming a trusted wisdom figure in the lives of his grandchildren, creating memorable moments with them, one on one. A heartwarming number of them are finding ways to live out the directive conveyed to Abraham in Genesis 12:2, "I will bless you ... so that you may be a blessing."

Some respondents felt they were sabotaging their dreams by caring for too much "stuff." George offered, "I think my possessions have possessed *me*, rather than the other way around. Too much time and money are being sucked up by maintenance of what I already have, so heaven knows I don't need more. I need smaller space, fewer things, a simpler life." He and his wife have committed themselves to the enormous task of sorting and selling and donating, determined to keep only those things they need and cherish.

Not all dreams are buried; some are borrowed. Several people expressed regret about dreams that they lived out as their own, but that actually belonged to someone else, usually their parents. One man said sadly, "I loved the outdoors and wanted to be a forest ranger, but I spent my life behind a desk. Now I'm going to make up for it by volunteering as a hiking guide at a boys' camp."

Tom felt he had been created to teach. Yet, he spent his career in more lucrative endeavors to provide the life he wanted for his family. He explained how he made peace with this unlived dream. "I had to find a way to honor that yearning and live it out in a different form, so I began to search for opportunities. Now I occasionally substitute teach at a local school; I teach a Sunday school class; I teach homeless men at the local community center how to apply for jobs and get a Social Security card. In my heart, I'm a teacher—what I was created to be."

If we're paying attention to God's natural process of growing more deeply into who we are in the later years, we will appreciate the sentiments expressed by writer Dawna Markova. On the night when her father died ("with a shrug," she says), she experienced a startling epiphany. In her opinion, her father had lived an uninteresting, small, safe, banal, fear-filled existence. She woke in the night with a start, sat up in bed, and thought, "I will not die an unlived life!" She vowed to live with her heart wide open, without fear "of falling or catching fire."[10]

So, dare to revisit old buried dreams and dust them off. Perhaps they can be salvaged in surprising new ways. Think outside the box. Take a chance. Above all, don't die with your music still in you.

Looking Inside

1. Think of yourself as you were at age thirty-five. What parts are still the same? What has changed in response to your life lessons?

2. Name one thing that has been part of your persona that doesn't conform to who you are in your true self.

3. Name three things that really "light your fire." What do they say about who you really are inside?

4. What spark of creativity within you needs an outlet? How can you expand and nurture that spark?

5. What dream of yours has never seen the light of day? How might you honor the dream, even if it can't be completely realized?

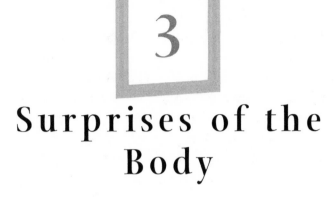

Surprises of the Body

Do you not know that your body is a temple of the Holy Spirit?... Therefore glorify God in your body.
1 CORINTHIANS 6:19, 20

It isn't only the cries of the soul that confront us in later life. The body, too, begins to demand a greater share of our attention. Sometimes the call becomes a shout; the twitch becomes a spasm; the ache explodes into a crescendo of pain. This once-friendly body can play the role of an enemy that is winning an imaginary battle. We often feel betrayed, rebellious, and terribly frustrated, as if a sinister force were taking over our physical bodies without our permission, and we barely recognize ourselves.

Ralph lightened the heaviness with humor. "I feel like an automobile whose warranty is expiring and the parts are beginning to malfunction, one by one," he said with a strained chuckle. On the other hand, Christina, when asked about her reactions to the body's decline, brightened with this comment: "I'm surprised that I have this much stamina and strength at age eighty. Who would have thought it?"

In some mysterious way, this diminishing control of our bodies points us toward something more stable. We ask ourselves, "Just who am I apart from this physical shell?" Yet, are we really separate? In facing the physical realities of later life, we tend to become more aware of the interconnectedness of our minds, bodies, and spirits. That intricacy can leave us awestruck and bewildered. As our once-reliable bodies slip from our control, we long for something that steadies the ground beneath us.

Regardless of what aches and pains come to visit, this sense of waning control threatens our independence and frightens us. The genetic codes we carry are more powerful than we expected. Yet, in spite of that, most seniors I know try to assume responsibility for whatever degree of control and maintenance are possible. For example, Alex deals with sky-high cholesterol numbers, struggling to outlive the predictable midlife death sentences of his male ancestors. He eats fruits and vegetables, walks daily, and is grateful for the wonders of modern medications.

I can't hide from my heritage either. I recognize my own female-pattern baldness in old photos of my mother and aunts and try to artfully comb my thinning hair over the bald spots. If I end up with a wig, so be it.

The thoughtful folks I interviewed had a ready supply of suggestions as well as lamentations. Many echoed the determination of one spunky senior who remarked, "I don't want to miss my life by feverishly maintaining my body!" In the variety of reactions I received to questions about the body, everyone seemed to be walking the tightrope between obsession and neglect, between careful concern and fretful worry. That balance isn't easy to find.

To be sure, this package of bones and blood that houses us is insistent that we take proper notice of it. Common sense tells us that the body's changes are a natural part of the aging process, but we're surprised when it actually happens to *us*.

Who Is That in the Mirror?

I think your whole life shows up in your face and you should be proud of that.

LAUREN BACALL

When I asked Charlotte what had surprised her most about growing older, she smiled timidly and said, "I've discovered that there's a little old lady that lives with me, and I spot her every time I pass the mirror!" The outer alterations of the body are usually the first things to be noticed by us as well as by others, reflected in such comments as "She's really looking her age," or "His gray hair makes him look distinguished." Even though we can count our own birthdays, from time to time we're shocked by what we see in the mirror, especially when we feel so young inside.

Have you noticed that Mother Nature tries to help us navigate this change in an unusual way? It's a fascinating kindness of nature that our eyesight declines as the imperfections increase, so we may be unaware of how dramatic our change of appearance actually is. In the bathroom mirror, without glasses, the wrinkles blur into imagined smoothness. Then along come bifocals—both a blessing and a curse. Overnight our faces turn into road maps, crisscrossed by tiny crevices and potholes—the price we pay for the ability to read small print.

Several years ago, I was compiling notes on the overall theme of letting go in preparation for a book on that topic. I uncovered an unexpected issue: the difficulty of letting go of the younger self—the self that we thought would always be unwrinkled, clearheaded, and robust. In *Necessary Losses*, Judith Viorst wrote of old age:

> We may start to feel that this is a time of always letting go, of one thing after another: our waistlines, our vigor, our sense of adventure, our 20/20 vision.... And as we acquire new aches and new pains, our health care is, of necessity, being supplied by internists, cardiologists, urologists,

periodontists, gynecologists and psychiatrists, from all of whom we want a second opinion ... one that says, "Don't worry, you are going to live forever."[1]

Men, too, bemoan this loss, using different contexts, of course. Max admitted that he was appalled by his appearance, citing varicose veins, peculiar splotches, unwelcome moles, and a paunchy midsection. Some are unhappy with the Yul Brynner look, choosing a toupee over a shiny pate. Some reach for Grecian Formula to camouflage the gray roots. Cosmetic surgery is capturing the fancy of many men, revealing that ego investment in appearance runs through both genders.

Our obsession with youth is not always about appearance, of course. Many seek out younger marriage partners, retain childish behaviors, or start running with a younger crowd. Others seem unable to move beyond their yearning to relive the high-school ball games, the college pranks, or the vocational successes and failures. No matter what picture of the past we cling to, we seem intent on slowing down the clock in whatever way we can.

The men I interviewed cited one bodily concern more often than appearance—that of limited stamina and diminished athletic prowess. They complained about everything from a loss of manual dexterity to a loss of muscle tone, all saying essentially the same thing: "I can't do what I used to do and I'm scared. I feel less of a man." Going down into deeper personal space revealed other concerns, such as "Will I end up as a permanent resident of my La-Z-Boy recliner, of use to no one?" "Will I be a burden to my kids, unable to bathe and dress myself?" "Why did God design it this way—this wasting away is humiliating!" Frightening prospects indeed.

Bruce's first response to his body's diminishment was, "I can't give in to this. I need to push my body, not succumb to it—I'll run a marathon!" He was, in effect, trying to outrun aging, if not by speed, then by endurance. A lifelong jogger, he launched into an exhaustive training regimen, determined to prove his prowess. "It was a huge mistake," he admitted. "About seven miles into the marathon when my body began to shout 'NO!' I tried to strike a deal with God: 'If you'll just let me get to the finish line still breathing and in one piece, I will never *ever* do this again.'" As he stumbled across the finish line in a daze, Bruce was grateful to have survived. He discovered he didn't want to be the poster boy for aging athletes and concluded with a smile, "I learned something, though—that there's a great deal of difference between courage and foolishness. And that I'm not bullet-proof after all."

My aunt Judy's bravado almost cost her a broken hip. Though in her nineties, she insisted on climbing the stairs to my second-floor apartment, refusing to ride the elevator chair. With teeth clenched, she virtually willed herself up each step. Then she declined to use her walker when she finally reached the second landing. Her body was yelling at her to slow down, hold on to the rail, and grab the walker. But her ego and false pride were egging her on, telling her she had to prove herself. When she inevitably stumbled, I caught her before she pitched backward. Barely.

In contrast to that, Carol decided to heed her body's cues. Normally a hyperactive bundle of energy, she began to experience a physical lull after lunch each day when she reached her late sixties. After weeks of trying to push through the fatigue, she described her change of heart (and routine) like this: "I decided to say '*Si* to siestas,'" she declared. "Now I get off my feet for a couple of hours, just as they do south of the border, and give my body what it wants—an afternoon rest. As a result, I have more energy for the evenings. Plus, I've read some really good books as I gave my mind a siesta as well."

Regardless of what we see in the mirror, through the aging process there is a sacred invitation to redefine our concept of beauty and appearance. The qualities of spiritual strength, integrity, and curiosity take on a certain radiance and magnetism. In fact, the best cosmetic may be a lively, inquiring mind and a countenance of compassion.

Listening to the Body's Wisdom

We've come a long way from the dualism of the Greeks, in which the body was seen as separate from the spirit. The elderly people who shared their opinions with me were aware that the intricate connections between body, mind, and spirit formed a very complex *whole*, a unified entity with a language all its own.

Yes, the body is constantly talking to us—with warnings, affirmations, and clues to divine guidance that is virtually built in to our created wiring. We ignore its unique language at our peril.

The problem is, we can't learn this lingo in the same way we learn Spanish, by memorizing nouns and conjugating verbs. We can understand it only through reflection, intuitive listening, and long-term observation. Another difficulty is, we can't learn it secondhand or by studying a generic text for Body-Speak 101. The instruction book has only one name on it—our own.

Before we decipher the meaning of the body's messages, we must first discover our particular body's signals of highs and lows, what I call our recurrent responses. Here are a few examples:

- Your head pounds. (Have I been in a noisy crowd for too long?)
- Your eyes burn. (Did that photo of the starving child affect me?)
- Your stomach turns over. (Is it the sight of the carnage in the TV report?)
- Your heart aches. (Can the death of my faithful Lab hurt this much?)
- Your jaw aches. (Have my teeth been clenched as a result of that disagreeable conversation?)
- You have bone-crushing fatigue. (Do I need more rest or more stimulation?)
- You lean forward, moving and breathing too fast. (Do I have a chronic case of "hurry sickness"?)
- And my personal favorite, a strange sore throat ... here's that story.

Years and years ago, an ear/nose/throat physician (who happened to be a friend and neighbor) introduced me to my body's primary emotional SOS. During times of great stress (of which I was largely unconscious), I kept showing up at his office, insisting that I had contracted strep throat from my small children and needed antibiotics pronto. My throat really, truly hurt. I could barely swallow. After examining my throat and declaring it free of all infection (I didn't believe him, of course), he pulled down a huge medical chart and taught me a life-changing lesson. I've never forgotten his prophetic words, uttered more than forty years ago:

"Linda, God has created every one of us with a stress signal to let us know that something is amiss. Yours seems to be esophageal spasms." As he pointed out the series of tiny muscles lining the esophagus, he added, "Remember exactly what this ache feels like. Notice it. Learn it. Listen to it. It's up to you to discover the causes. Maybe you're not saying things you need to say, and the words are 'stuck in your throat.' Maybe fear is lodging there. All I know is this: if you learn to heed its warnings, you can choose to change whatever needs changing before your body does it for you."

What an incredible gift. Unfortunately, we tend to ignore this astounding internal guidance system while pursuing the will of God through intellectual means. We try to figure things out in our heads rather than experiencing them in our hearts and bodies. It's much easier to reflect and observe and discuss, rather than actually commit to the tedious work of acting on the vital information shouted by our own cells.

Once you have discovered your natural recurrent responses, dig a little deeper. Notice the specific reactions that prompt the response, which means paying close attention to any emotional surge that occurs in your body. Name the feeling: anger, impatience, exhilaration, ecstasy, despair, delight, sorrow, tension, anxiety. Pay attention to involuntary tears, which always carry significant messages. Have the courage to ask, "What inside me is reacting involuntarily and why?" "Is there a heartache beneath this headache?"

The best tool I've ever engaged for singling out these emotional reactions is the age-old daily examen, a practice of honest self-examination that explores the events and behaviors of the day in an effort to discern their spiritual significance. This particular version of the practice facilitates a deepening knowledge of our wiring.

Spiritual Practice: Examen
At the end of the day, ask yourself these questions:

- What caused me to smile today?
- What touched or moved me to tears today?
- What inspired me today?
- What was "life-giving" to me today?
- What felt "life-taking" to me today?
- When did I feel a burst of energy today?
- What sparked my curiosity today?
- What did I learn about God and about myself today?

Once you've explored your responses and reactions, you can count on some serious pushback in many forms of resistance. Blaming and justifying usually show up first: "If they hadn't said that, I wouldn't be so irritated." "I have every right to be angry after what she did to me." "Every time he's late, I get so annoyed it spoils my whole evening!" We begin to blame, defend ourselves, and get so overwhelmed with the emotion that we can't make wise choices about what action to take. We can do little about someone else's behavior. We can, however, decide not to be poisoned by our own reactions. Then we can decide how to diffuse the toxicity in our own bodies. Otherwise, we act out the equivalent of drinking hemlock and expecting the other person to get sick.

In our conversation, Constance pointed out that pain and resistance are often bedfellows. Her active life was blown apart by a rare eye disease that not only robbed her of independence but left her unable to engage in her favorite activity—reading.

She counseled, "When I fight my disease or get angry because it keeps me from doing what I want to do, I allow myself to feel those feelings fully, then move beyond them. I've found that a saner choice is to stop the negative complaints and breathe away the resistance. Then I focus on what I can still do, rather than what I can't. Believe me, the pragmatic, problem-solving part of me has really gotten a workout in dealing with this illness!"

She checked out books on tape from the library, invested in an iPod and a high-powered magnifying glass, and sang along with her recordings of familiar hymns. A "giver" by nature, she tackled the tough task of learning to receive, asking specifically for what she needed and not expecting others to read her mind. Through it all, Constance has relied on her solid faith foundation and a praying community of friends to convey the love of God to her in both tangible and intangible ways.

We need to observe how our bodies register not only resistance but resonance as well. When something is congruent with our values, authentic to our souls, and affirming of who we are, how does the body feel? There's no "one size fits all." Each person tends to have a definition peculiar to his or her body and experience:

- An internal sigh of contentment
- A feeling of harmony and peace
- An affirmation of the spirit
- A sense of life's gentle flow
- A glow of delight
- A surge of euphoria
- A relaxing resonance in the diaphragm
- A surprising smile
- A sensation inside that says *yes*

Can we misread physical messages? Of course. Can we misinterpret the body language of others? You bet. Do we then relegate the wisdom of the body to a secondary status? Too often, we do just that, going to the opposite extreme and dismissing the body's feedback as unreliable and capricious. In doing so, we turn our backs on one of the most powerful messengers our Creator has provided. This is not to say "If it feels good, do it" or to obey every imagined yearning as a call for action. Rather, it invites us to pay attention to the responses of our physical nature, explore our reactions, discover the resistance, realize the resonance, and then decide if and how to act it out.

Listen to your body's cues. Respect them. Interact with them. And above all, hallow them as an avenue through which the loving nurture and guidance of God come to you.

Coping with Pain and Illness

"Pain makes theologians of us all," writes Barbara Brown Taylor in *An Altar in the World*. She goes on to say, "If you have spent even one night in real physical pain, then you know what that can do to your faith in God, not to mention your faith in your own ability to manage your life."[2]

Barbara was careful not to romanticize or dismiss pain as insignificant. "The next time you are in real pain," she writes, "see how you feel about television shows, new appliances, a clean house, or your resume.... All that will do anything for you is some cool water, held out by someone who has stopped everything else in order to look after you. An extra blanket might also help, a dry pillow, the simple knowledge that there is someone in the house who might hear you if you cried."[3] In chronicling her own experience with pain, she found herself "turning away from the 'God in charge of pain removal' toward the 'God who had stayed with me through the pain no matter what I said.'"[4] Most of the seniors I spoke with echoed her sentiments.

The challenging pathway through pain and illness seems to follow a fascinating trajectory of experience, moving from *resisting and hating* the pain to *accepting and hallowing* the pain, and then finally to *handling* the pain. This movement from breakdown to breakthrough is particularly noticeable in dealing with chronic conditions.

Pain and suffering, inherent in the human condition, shrink our universe and force our focus to a pinpoint—and of course we resist it. Who wouldn't? We don't like it; we beg God to get us out of it; it shatters our illusion of control. Troublesome questions come to call: What did I do to deserve this? Why didn't I take better care of myself? If I pray hard enough, will God take it away? Where did I go wrong? Why, why, why?

An inherent sense of entitlement rears its selfish head. (I've tried to be a good person all my life, and this is what I get?) We take scriptures out of context and concretize them—"The wages of sin is death" (Romans 6:23) or "Ask and you shall receive" (John 16:24) or "The Lord watches over the way of the righteous, but the way of the wicked will perish" (Psalms 1:6). This unconscious reasoning is even reflected in the bedside comments we make: "He is such a wonderful man—no way he deserved this," or "I know God will heal her because she's been a loyal Christian all her life."

Margie even wondered whether she had some complicity in her condition, whether it was somehow her fault. Maybe it struck randomly for no apparent reason or was merely an accident. No matter what the cause, we often react with guilt, assuming some control we never actually had. The narrative inside us may ramble irrationally: "Maybe I'm being punished for that terrible thing I did twenty years ago" or "If only I had waited until after rush hour, I wouldn't have been involved in the automobile pileup." To the question "Why?" we add "What if?" As Margie described this stage of her illness, she concluded, "I realized that painful experiences are part of the package, that it isn't a matter of why or if, but *when*."

As we move through this minefield of emotions—from the self-centeredness that is a natural outgrowth of pain to the cosmic questions of why bad things happen to good people—it's a good idea to do so slowly and deliberately. Too often we assume that a true faith response is a stoic, grin-and-bear-it approach to suffering. Don't we usually reward this suppression of emotion as "He's amazing—never complains," or "She's so brave that she refuses pain medication"?

At some point, however, God invites us to move toward what may seem impossible: a *hallowing* of the pain. To hallow, to make holy, is to open yourself to the possibility that the physical diminishment may reveal something of the Divine, a treasure, a golden nugget of growth, if you are open to seeing it. Perhaps it is like the biblical story of Jacob wrestling with the angel. Jacob wouldn't let the angel go until he received its blessing, until the meaning of the encounter was revealed. Remember that Jacob went away from that all-night wrestling match not only with a physical wound—a limp—but also with a new name, a new purpose, a new blessing (Genesis 32:27–28). In asking, "What golden threads can I pull from this mess?" we embrace the pain as our teacher.

There's a difference between pain and suffering. Pain is a response of the body; suffering is a response of the mind. Try reaching for meaning without judgment or resentment, if it will allow the mind to help the body cope with pain.

If, however, our minds enter the faulty theological territory of "God caused this to move me forward spiritually," we can end up in unspoken bitterness and guilt. Responding with integrity essentially lets go of the cause and affirms the truth: "All things work together for those who love God" (Romans 8:28).

The familiar analogy posed by writer Flora Wuellner feels resonant to me. I wrote about it a few years ago:

> My favorite analogy for the role of tragedy in our lives is a simple one I heard in 1993 from author Flora Wuellner during one of her instruction periods at the Academy for Spiritual Formation. My paraphrase goes like this: "It's one thing to say that if my child falls down the concrete stairs and breaks his leg, I as a good parent will do everything in my power to bring something good out of that experience—I'll read to him, teach him that he shouldn't have

left his rollerblades at the top of the stairs, help him heal, love him through the experience of pain and recovery. However, it's quite another thing to say that as a good parent, I would PUSH that child down the stairs in order that he can learn those valuable lessons!"[5]

God is willing to love and nurture us through whatever experience catapulted us to the bottom of the stairs. Hallowing our pain and diminishment through acceptance and a willingness to grow is tough work. But it can usher us into a new state of being—a larger life spiritually, even if we are living a smaller life physically.

Jim was dealing with the early stages of Parkinson's disease. As he finally moved toward acceptance of his condition, he encountered some surprising changes in his theology of how God could bless him through his experience. His preconceived notions of control, divine justice, and God's protection changed. They expanded beyond his own private world. He lost the sense of entitlement that God would treat him better than anyone else, and in its place, a genuine solidarity with fellow sufferers developed. The sensation was not simply a concept, but grew into a compassion born out of his own flesh-and-blood, in-your-face experience. It was like a graduate course in patience, endurance, and hope. He printed out one of his favorite scripture verses and placed it on his desk:

> Suffering produces endurance, and endurance produces character, and character produces hope, and hope does not disappoint us, because God's love has been poured into our hearts through the Holy Spirit that has been given to us (Romans 5:3).

Many seniors told me inspiring stories of practical ways that they chose to handle the pain and isolation of long periods of recovery. They planned ahead instead of after the fact. Some learned deep breathing techniques and meditation practices to aid them in dealing with postoperative pain. They took the initiative in responding to offers of help by telling friends exactly what they needed, whether it was a ride to the hospital, grocery store errands, or help with pets. Some made a list of favorite foods for those who wanted to supply meals.

Michelle knew she would be mostly bedridden during her convalescence from extensive surgery on both feet. So she made some concrete plans in an attempt to make the time more than a boring, unproductive stretch of endurance. She assembled boxes of photos that had been gathering dust for years and bought albums and supplies for organizing them. She made a list of old friends she had neglected to contact, jotting down their addresses and phone numbers before her surgery so they would be handy during her confinement. Her cleanup goal was to go through one drawer a day—from the kitchen to the bedroom—until they were neat and tidy. All the preparations helped her move into the surgery with a more positive attitude, as she squeezed every ounce of possible productivity out of the experience.

One ambitious senior resolved to master the wonders of his laptop computer during his confinement, asking a friend to tutor him an hour or so a day. He even downloaded Skype (a simple computer application for interactive visual communication) so that he could keep in closer contact with his out-of-state grandchildren. A woman with artistic interests assembled books and music CDs to divert her attention and help her focus on something besides her discomfort.

There's no doubt that, as Barbara Brown Taylor cleverly put it, "Living with daily pain is a high-maintenance relationship."[6] Doctors and nurses, friends and family can offer to assist us, but often they don't know specifically what we need. When we can say, "Would you please bring me the utensil drawer to the left of the stove and put it here on the bed?" it's a win-win, plus you'll love looking at the order you've created.

Underneath all these creative coping mechanisms lies an attitude that reflects the famous words of medieval mystic woman

Julian of Norwich in the fourteenth century, "All shall be well, and all manner of things shall be well."[7] It may be necessary, however, to broaden and redefine what we mean by *well*, resting in radical trust that, though we can't always be cured, we can be healed.

Libido and Longevity

Philosopher Eknath Easwaran had this clever observation of the power of libido in our lives: "Desire is neutral. Like electricity, it can either light the home or electrocute the tenant."[8]

You may be surprised that I'm including this topic in a book about the lives of seniors, but the feedback I received to one question demanded that I not omit it. When I asked, "Is there something about aging that you haven't told anyone?" I discovered that the elephant in the room was sex.

More than half of those I interviewed declined to answer that question or dismissed it as irrelevant. The first person to give me a completely honest answer was a man of seventy who got a faraway look in his eyes as he answered truthfully, "I no longer hope that an attractive woman will be seated next to me on an airline flight." It was difficult to hide my surprise as he added, "Women seem to regard me as a father figure now. Makes me a little sad. Not that I would act on my interest, mind you, but I really enjoy and appreciate women."

Eighty-year-old Lily almost whispered her response to the same question. "I've never told anyone this, but I would like to have sex one more time before I die," she confided with a blush. A great majority of those who related secret thoughts talked about some aspect of sexuality. This particular generation of adults was brought up in a context where this life-affirming, God-given part of our nature was strictly a taboo subject. Many of us remember our parents using the term *in a family way* rather than daring to speak the word *pregnant*. That said, you can imagine the puritanical rules surrounding other aspects of the subject.

Surprise number two: contrary to prevailing opinion, the comments were not predictable by gender. The responses of both men and women ran the gamut from virtually no libido to a heightened sexual interest. This presented particular challenges in long-term marriages.

One very thoughtful answer came from a woman in her early seventies, who had always valued the sexual side of her marriage. "My hormones must have run out," she said. "My interest has declined sharply in the last few years. Strange thing, though … even though I'm less interested in sex, I'm more interested in my spouse as a person than I ever have been before. We appreciate each other and have a deeper intimacy than we did in those young, high-hormone days."

Others expressed similar feelings. As sex moved aside as the focus of their relationship, they began to notice the value of their shared history, mutual interests, and meaningful contacts with adult children and grandchildren. There was a general consensus about the importance of good, honest communication in marriages where one partner was more interested in sex than the other. "The key to handling the problem of differing needs," advised one woman, "is the ability to talk it out without accusation." That and a willingness to find a compromise to accommodate each other's needs.

I couldn't discover a norm among seniors on the topic of sex. About the time I thought I detected a pattern of diminished desire, I would encounter comments such as this one from a man in his eighties: "My wife and I have the most satisfying physical relationship now than we've ever had. The kids are gone, we know and love each other deeply, and we're free at last to be honeymooners."

There was one pervasive conclusion that came through loud and clear. People still enjoyed the company and attraction of the opposite sex, whether it was physically expressed or not. Many seniors discovered broader aspects of their sexuality and delighted in companionship. Their sentiments seemed to suggest that they regarded sex as the icing, not the "cake." Clearly, the cake is about love in all its manifestations—kindness, companionship, appreciation, and deep affection.

Yet there were a number of responses that affirmed the possibility of powerful romantic late-life love with a youthful vitality. "There's nothing quite like falling in love—at any age!" remarked one senior. "There's this rush of energy, the brilliant aliveness, the spontaneous delight, the joy of enjoying a concert sitting side by side, or merely being in comfortable silence with each other." Another person indicated that the internal chatter is somewhat the same at seventy as it was at seventeen. When will the phone ring? Should I wear the blue dress that matches my eyes? Should I clear my calendar for the weekend in case he asks me out? Or, does she really like me? Should I bring flowers? Does she think I'm too old?

They all agreed, however, that one thing is different. "When you're older," one person offered, "you consider some deeper issues. Do we see the world through the same lens? Can we share our past relationship successes and failures with complete safety, with no condemnation or judgment? Can we make jokes about my varicose veins or his double chin without diminishing each other?"

Spiritually mature adults usually know the difference between wanting a romantic partner and needing one. In healthy late-life relationships, you're free to choose the connection because it is meaningful, not because you need it to complete you as a person. One very wise woman with stars in her eyes reported, "He *gets it* about me, and I *get it* about him. Now *that's* the cake. If he brings flowers, that's definitely delicious icing. But we don't want to merge into each other's lives; each of us has a life of our own. We're like two whole people facing in the same direction—holding hands, maybe—but also standing shoulder to shoulder on equal footing."

It's never too late for love. The gift of sexuality that is so embedded in our nature by the Creator is always capable of expression, even as the years mount up. As one eighty-one-year-old gentleman said wistfully, "I still want a mate to share the last lap with me."

Are Limitations Limiting You?

Tiny and wrinkled as a prune at ninety-seven, Rose had a spinal curvature that formed a noticeable arc. But her spunk and spirit seemed as ramrod straight as they were at thirty-five. When our conversation turned to the topic of coping with limitations of the body, she remarked emphatically, "My dear, you can't let limitations limit you!" So what do we do in the wake of conditions that are not life-threatening, but definitely life-changing?

Frances revealed that bravery is not confined to the battlefield. I knew I was in for some tough, gritty advice when I met her. She had been battling a back condition for years and had sought the best medical advice possible. A physical therapist by profession, she had reached the limits of medical intervention and was looking at the rest of her life with serious chronic pain as her companion. Her opening words to me were, "Maybe my back can't get better, but my attitude can. I'm tired of hearing myself complain. I can either let pain rule my life, or I can try to find a way to rule the pain."

It is a work in progress for Frances. Her words were so determined and eloquent that I quote them here in full:

It seems to me that those of us with chronic pain have two possible avenues. One is give in to the pain and cease to live. The other is to take the pain with us and go out into life. Either way, the pain is there, but we miss so much of life if we completely give in to it. In the beginning, we make the choice each day, but pretty soon the way we have chosen becomes a way of approaching life, a habit. If we have chosen to surrender to the pain, it becomes harder and harder to reverse that choice. By the same token, if we have chosen to enjoy living in spite of the pain, surrender is not really an option anymore.

Maybe I was lucky because my pain started when I was still working full time and didn't have much of a choice; I *had* to work. By the time I was free to choose, the habit of living with the pain was locked in. Besides, I found that my pain was less when I was interacting with people and that I usually had a choice as to what to focus on. As the pain has become more severe, I have stuck with my original choice, tempered with a healthy dose of common sense.

My decision now is what *part* of living I will choose each day. When the pain is intense, there are certain things that are no longer an option, such as walking long distances. But I can do other forms of exercise. Plus, I can still walk short distances, if I sit down intermittently, let my back recover, then get up again. I've changed the way I travel, too. I haven't totally stopped, but I've found that if I drive instead of fly, I can take my foam mattresses with me. I can't do yard work, but I can still do some housework. However, I do not plan ever again in my life to get down on the floor to clean baseboards.

As I get older, the choices are more limited, of course, but I'm still clinging to my right to choose. It's up to me to decide responsibly when to concede to the pain when the cost is too high. Some things are not worth it. Others are worth it no matter how much pain it causes. For instance, I had dreamed for years of attending an Academy for Spiritual Formation, but it was a commitment of one week every three months for two years, and I couldn't see that far ahead, physically or financially. But despite all of that, I finally decided to defy the odds and go for it. It was really hard at first—sitting through lectures, standing during hymns, sleeping on a regular bed—but I kept making adjustments until I found a way to do it.

First, I promised myself I would take responsibility for my own pain without some unconscious cry for sympathy or personal concessions. I loaded a special chair, oversized heating pads, foam mattresses, and assorted other necessary gear into my car and drove the three hours two and from the meeting site. With no apologies, I stood when I could and sat when I couldn't. The loving-kindness of the community has surrounded me with support and encouragement and unspeakable joy. The experience has changed my life.

Those who deal creatively with their limitations do what Frances did—change their attitudes first. They begin to view the limitations as the realistic circumstances of their lives, rather than as a punishment or burden. If you think about it, most of us have performed this kind of attitude adjustment at earlier stages of life. For instance, when our children were born, our personal freedoms were curtailed, but we still were able to uncover rich opportunities for satisfaction.

In responding to the question "What have you discovered about yourself that you didn't notice before?" one man in his nineties replied, "I didn't realize that I possessed an underlying sense of optimism about life and about people. I had no idea how valuable it would be in shaping these last years."

Quite a number of honest seniors confided that they were making an effort to curtail their conversation about their "ailment of the week." Henry said, "I've learned that life isn't an 'organ recital' and that when I tell people way more than they want to hear about my aches and pains, I become boring—even to other seniors. My family gets tired of my bellyaching about the things I can't do anymore. They just want me to focus on what I can still do. I've come to believe that one of the best legacies we can leave our children is a role model of positive aging, and I'm committed to that."

Ethel was a self-starter by nature, and that trait served her well when she found herself virtually bedridden in her late eighties. Her mind, however, hadn't aged at the same rate as her body, so she decided the best way to deal with her limitations was to champion a project. She approached her church leaders about a ministry to shut-ins that she could single-handedly operate from her bedroom. First, she got a church directory and asked that they mark all shut-ins in the congregation, along with addresses and phone numbers. Next, she requested particulars about their specific needs and situations. Armed with all this information she pledged to call each shut-in once a week, chat with them, check on their circumstances, and send a brief report to the church staff. But Ethel was just getting started. In addition, she bought several boxes of cheerful cards and a book of stamps so that the shut-ins could receive messages of encouragement from their church community that they could read and reread. Ethel even included the weekly church bulletin to provide more connection to the life of the church.

Limitations threatened to disturb Marvin's daily routine in a different way. When I interviewed him, it was obvious that he loved books—serious books. Tome after leather-bound tome lined the shelves from floor to ceiling in his den. He wasn't having any trouble with his eyesight, he reported, but his mental focus turned to a muddy malaise after a half hour or so. "I can't seem to read a whole book anymore," he said with a sigh. "It's as if some gremlin has stolen my ability to concentrate. I fought it for a while, but sheer determination didn't do the job. So I've switched to newspapers, short stories, and magazines, and I'm not quite so frustrated." These may seem to be small adaptations, but when habits of sixty or seventy years' duration must be changed, it takes an amazing amount of acceptance and flexibility.

Angie's grandchildren were her angels in disguise. With youthful candor and enthusiasm, they nudged her into an unusual way to deal with her limitations. When her macular degeneration and failing memory began to take an increasing toll on her active life, she was in a constant state of losing things and searching for the right lists. Her techie grands marched in one day with a brand-new computer and minced no words about why they were there. Plugging wires in every direction, they announced, "Granny, we have something important to teach you. This computer is really good at searching, and you're not. It's also good at remembering, and you're not. Get ready to meet your new best friend!"

A Spiritual Practice: Breath Prayer

Sometimes in dealing positively with limitations, we need a spiritual practice to undergird our practical efforts. One of the most challenging parts of the spiritual life is balancing honesty and hope. The "It is as it is" breath prayer helps bring us back to our heart center, where we can be reminded that we're not in this alone.[9]

When you find yourself on a downward spiral of "poor me," break the pattern with an abrupt deep breath, saying simply, "It is as it is; I accept it." Then continue to inhale and exhale, breathing in the empowering love of God and breathing out the desperation. This prayer can provide the impetus to shift from pain to possibility and plunge you right smack into the present moment.

Yesterday's history can't be rewritten, but this prayer can at least open our hearts to tomorrow's hope. There's little doubt that lamenting *what used to be* saps our energy for dealing with *what is*.

And while we're at it, let's add a prayer of thanksgiving that modern science and technology are such incredible allies in the process of aging. Whether it's a pacemaker or a hearing aid, cataract surgery or a bionic hip, we have more reason than ever before to look Father Time squarely in the eyes and say, "Let's be pals."

At this later stage of life, we can more clearly realize that the body is not just a shell to encase the soul. It's intertwined with the workings of the mind and spirit—a miraculous network. We are invited to ask ourselves, "How shall I treat it, use it, care for it, understand it?" This spiritual surprise can lead us to regard our bodies as more than a burden to bear.

Looking Inside

1. How has your attitude toward your appearance changed as you age?

2. What is your body's stress signal? What is your usual response to it?

3. Think of someone you know who copes with pain and illness in a realistic, hopeful way. What seems to be the source of his strength? How can you apply her example to your own life?

4. How much time do you spend grumbling about what you can no longer do? How do others react to your complaints?

5. Make a list of the activities you can still enjoy and the tasks you can still perform.

Surprises in
Relationships

*I love you not only for what you are, but for who I am when
I am with you.*
ANONYMOUS

As Lester reflected on his experience of surprise in later life, he remarked, "I find myself paying closer attention to the quality of my relationships—all of them. Time is short, and I'm no longer willing to spend much time with folks I don't really care about or who don't care about me. I'm interested in honest relationships where I can be myself."

His wife, Donna, agreed. "Some of my friendships are one-sided," she said thoughtfully. "It's clear that one person cares more about being friends than the other does. I'm allowing those relationships to fade away naturally. And another thing—no more hanging out with people who bring out the worst in me!"

As we shift gears in our senior years, virtually all our relationships shift in response to this different stage of life, including our connections to friends, partners, adult children, the world, and the Holy. We celebrate the presence of loved ones in our lives and grieve when we lose them. We react to the changes in others, as they react to the changes in us. Some relationships grow deeper; some become more distant. But one thing is certain: they do shift.

Friends Who Feed Your Soul

No one has greater love than this, to lay down one's life for one's friends.

JOHN 15:13

We are born into our families, but we choose our friends. And like the proverbial "balm in Gilead" (Jeremiah 8:22), they soothe our souls, often filling in the painful gaps left unfulfilled in other personal attachments. Friendship is the jack-of-all-trades of relationships.

I like philosopher George Santayana's writings on the categories of friendship that show the depth of their diversity. He wrote that "friendship is almost always the union of a part of one mind with a part of another; people are friends in spots."

- We have convenience friends, whose lives routinely intersect with ours.
- We have special-interest friends with whom we share a particular activity.
- We have historical friends, who knew us way back when.
- We have crossroads friends who shared a life event with us or were coworkers.
- We have cross-generational friends, where the wisdom of one generation enlivens the other.
- We have family friends (not friends *of* the family, but friends *in* the family).
- We have spiritual friends who help us along our spiritual journey.
- We have soul friends with whom we have a mysterious connection for no discernible reason.

- And, if we're lucky, we have close friends, whose special
  bond transcends time and space—friends we can call
  at three in the morning when we're feeling scared or
  sick or out of sorts.

Sometimes when we're struggling in the dark, we need someone
to hold the lamp for us until we can pick it up again. Some friends
aren't all things to us, nor are we to them, but their value is not
diminished.

Jane spoke about her need to be around people who nurture
her spirit. "I notice how I feel inside when I'm with certain friends,
and how my body feels…. Do I feel better after I've been around
them or worse? Am I energized or drained? Encouraged or discouraged? If I can, I limit my time with those who make me feel
smaller and starve my soul. That doesn't mean I don't choose to
be with friends who are sick and grieving just because it makes me
sad; that feels authentic, *real*, to be with those who need me. I
want to be there for them. I'm talking about situations where I'm
constantly swallowing words or opinions, or trying to be something I'm not—you know, 'pretend' friendships."

Cora echoed the same sentiment in colorful language. "If
I can help it, I'm not staying in relationships or settings that
kill my spirit and leach the very life out of me," she said. "It's
like getting pecked to death by a duck!"

Scott mentioned his growing appreciation of his men
friends. "I've worked hard all my life and felt that any leisure time
should be devoted to my family. Now that I'm retired, it's such a
pleasure to have unhurried conversations with other men and
develop bonds of friendship."

This outlook was replicated by a number of seniors in a
retirement community as they described the joy of living with
others in the same boat. "We're peers," remarked one animated
gentleman. "Sure, sometimes we commiserate with each other,
but we also offer encouragement. And one of the best things is
that no one ignores us or treats us like old geezers to be tolerated

rather than talked to!" Another added, "Before I moved here, the TV was my constant companion, my electronic buddy. I watched sports I didn't even like and (I'm ashamed to say) I had begun to think of the actors on *As the World Turns* as friends of mine. Here in this place, I have real flesh-and-blood pals, and it's great."

Alice brought up the value of friends who had the courage to be absolutely honest with her. To that comment, I say, "Ditto." I was reminded of the value of candor just last evening while having dinner with an old friend. In the midst of my familiar litany of excuses for being woefully behind on this very manuscript that you're reading, she narrowed her eyes into slits and said emphatically, "Enough excuses, Linda. You've wanted to write on this subject for years, and now you have the opportunity to do it. So do it!" Lest she seem like an ogre, I'll add that later she offered gently, "Now what can I do to help you stay on track?"

We all need friends who will jerk a knot in us when we need it. It's an abrupt reminder that someone cares more about us than the friendship, meaning that they love us enough to risk our anger by telling it like it is, for our own good. Longtime friends usually recognize our tired patterns of procrastination and diversion and some of them aren't afraid to tell us so. Of course, challenging words to and from friends can be acts of kindness *only* when spoken in an atmosphere of safety and mutual vulnerability. For me, that kind of honesty is a gift beyond measure.

As the years pass and time shrinks, we tend to become more particular about those whom we call our friends, especially in difficult times. In the words of actress Arlene Francis, "Trouble is a sieve through which we sift our acquaintances. Those too big to pass through are our friends."

Moreover, we evaluate our friendships with a measuring stick of deeper values. Excerpts from the poignant words of "The Invitation," written by Oriah Mountain Dreamer, a Canadian teacher and author, give a poetic picture of this:

It doesn't interest me what you do for a living.
I want to know what you ache for
and if you dare to dream of meeting your heart's longing.

It doesn't interest me how old you are.
I want to know if you will risk looking like a fool
for love
for your dream
for the adventure of being alive.

It doesn't interest me what planets are squaring your moon ...
I want to know if you have touched the centre of your own sorrow
if you have been opened by life's betrayals
or have become shrivelled and closed
from fear of further pain.

I want to know if you can sit with pain
mine or your own
without moving to hide it
or fade it
or fix it.

I want to know if you can be with joy
mine or your own
if you can dance with wildness
and let the ecstasy fill you to the tips of your
    fingers and toes
without cautioning us
to be careful
to be realistic
to remember the limitations of being human.

It doesn't interest me if the story you are telling me is true.
I want to know if you can
disappoint another

to be true to yourself.
If you can bear the accusation of betrayal
and not betray your own soul.
If you can be faithless
and therefore trustworthy.

I want to know if you can see Beauty
even when it is not pretty
every day.
And if you can source your own life
from its presence.

I want to know if you can live with failure
yours and mine
and still stand at the edge of the lake
and shout to the silver of the full moon,
"Yes."

It doesn't interest me
to know where you live or how much money you have.
I want to know if you can get up
after the night of grief and despair
weary and bruised to the bone
and do what needs to be done
to feed the children.

It doesn't interest me who you know
or how you came to be here.
I want to know if you will stand
in the centre of the fire
with me
and not shrink back.

It doesn't interest me where or what or with whom
you have studied.

I want to know what sustains you
from the inside
when all else falls away.

I want to know if you can be alone
with yourself
and if you truly like the company you keep
in the empty moments.[1]

Renegotiating Partnerships

Carla repeated a phrase I had heard many times, "I married him for better or for worse, but not for *lunch!*" This familiar stab at humor tries to soften the trauma of two people trying to live together as their customary roles are tossed into the air. When those identities fall back to earth, they're all scrambled up and need to be sorted all over again.

Marriages, especially long ones, demand periodic reshufflings of the roles through the years:

- The honeymoon ends, and day-to-day reality sets in.
- A baby is born, and so is sleep deprivation.
- Teenagers get involved, and leisurely Saturdays are stuffed with wall-to-wall activities.
- Grandparents become ill, and caretaking is added to the full routine.
- The kids leave for college, and silence settles in.
- One of the spouses develops health problems, and the other assumes the unfamiliar role of caregiver in the relationship.
- Retirement suddenly places two people together 24/7.

With every new life stage comes a renegotiation of the relationship. Carla shook her head in frustration as she continued her comments about the transition of retirement. "Whether employed or not, the kitchen has always been my domain, a kind of refuge for me because I love to cook. Now that Al is home with too much time on his hands, I feel as if my space is being invaded. When I spied him alphabetizing my spices, I knew we were in trouble. Thank goodness we had sense enough to stop and renegotiate our relationship before our home became a battleground. Both of us seemed to be unconsciously vying for territory."

And there seems to be plenty of territory to defend in such situations—space, responsibilities, intimacy, privacy. And once again, the key to success was clear, open, honest communication—plus ongoing flexibility and a genuine willingness to listen to each other without fixing, without judgment, without defending, without interrupting, without behaving like martyrs.

The seniors I interviewed were eager to give advice on how to travel this terrain in a positive way so that neither partner ends up winning or losing. Here are some of their tips for this transition:

- Commit to the process of working it out rather than battling it out.
- Clear the slate; leave the past out of it and don't bring up old behaviors; accept each other as you are now where you are now, not as you were then.
- Speak clearly and honestly; don't hint around and expect the other person to guess what you mean. And no interrupting.
- Own up to your feelings and frustrations—no pretending, no blaming. Use phrases such as "I feel ..." rather than "You make me feel ..."
- Instead of hiding things that can fester and become poisonous to either of you, give each other the safety and acceptance that can cushion honesty.
- Refrain from engaging in an emotional ping-pong match of defensiveness; one person may throw down the gauntlet, but you don't have to pick it up.

- Realize that true compromise involves conflict, but you can still be yourself and allow the other to do the same.
- You don't need to be joined at the hip; retain separate interests as well as projects and activities you can share. You're not trying to mesh your lives; you're attempting to march into the future as two whole people—hand in hand.
- Listen—really listen—without rushing to judgment. In the words of writer and teacher Robert Benson, "Sometimes being listened to is so much like love, you can't tell the difference."[2]

Walter is a poignant example of the need to adapt to sudden situations. When his previously healthy wife suffered a stroke, his life was turned upside down overnight. Once he accepted the situation, he resolved to enter the caretaking role with as much creativity as possible. Though somewhat impaired, Laura wasn't totally confined to bed. So they decided to record their memoirs for the grandchildren through print and recordings and had a wonderful time reviewing old photo albums and remembering events together. Each of them composed an "Emotional Will" in the form of advice, appreciation, and memories to pass down to their offspring. They wanted this mutual task of honoring their past to provide a sense of family continuity.

Another couple, who had been lifelong gardeners, had to move to a small apartment in a retirement home with no outlet for their green thumbs. They transformed their kitchen windows into a beautiful shelf garden, growing herbs and flowers that they could tend daily. They planted seeds and shared the bounty with friends. Soon the front steps of the community home were brightened with pots of seasonal flowers. They took what seemed to be lost and transformed it into gain.

John and Julia had a tough time with their late-life relationship negotiations. After the children and their families moved to different parts of the country and retirement placed them alone in their home, their dysfunctional relationship was staring them squarely in the face. Without the buffers of careers and children, there was nowhere to hide.

John offered, "Our buried frustration with each other was so toxic that we almost didn't make it." Tempers flared off and on for weeks, months. Julia became so committed to total honesty that she wasn't willing to let any irritating comment pass. Her anger at her husband's impatience and diminishing comments had been boiling beneath the surface for years. John described how he fought back: "I felt battered and began to spew venom of my own." Their heated exchanges were emotional explosions that threatened their long marriage.

But they continued to hang on, determined to either craft an honest relationship or get a divorce. After damaging, defensive language on both their parts, they agreed on some healthy boundaries. They used words such as, "I refuse to stay in this room when you speak to me in an attacking manner," or "Remember, we've agreed not to interrupt each other, but to listen before speaking." I'm happy to report that once all the spleen was vented, they began to recall the things they had in common (besides five children) and the joy they had in each other's company. They examined their minuses, then made a mutual decision to build on their pluses. As their focus moved to the things they liked about each other, each began to soften the behaviors that irritated the other. Because they had spoken their frustrations openly, their awareness moved them toward compromise and genuine commitment. They remembered why they married each other in the first place.

Some stories don't have such a happy ending. Occasionally, couples who enter this process of honest negotiation can't discover enough commonality on which to rebuild their relationship. But for those who want to find ways to repair the damage and save the marriage, the effort is well worth the bruised egos and frayed nerves. Forgiveness and faith are vital factors in the renegotiation of these important partnerships. They help us manage our warring emotions.

Adult Children: To Speak or Not to Speak

Matt put it bluntly, "What has surprised me is that the welfare of my kids is still front and center in my life. I assumed they would be on their own when they passed eighteen, but to tell the truth, the older they get, the bigger the problems are. Makes me wish they were three again so I could just fix it with a Band-Aid."

Another articulate senior put it this way: "You never really get over being Papa to your kids. You may think you've let them go, but it's an illusion. Just let them face a divorce or get into financial distress, and it's as if they're back in the playpen. That instinct to make it better and be the parental rescuer comes rushing back like a hurricane, and it trumps logic almost every time." Then he added thoughtfully, "I'm trying to learn about setting boundaries around that powerful paternal urge. It's hard for me to know when to let Papa Bear out of his cage and when to lock him up."

Many seniors found great joy in healthy relationships with their adult children, building satisfying grown-up friendships. On the other hand, some felt the term "adult children" was a contradiction in terms, forming the basis for conflict. They are always your children, though mature in years, and often the rules of the relationship are murky at best. Paul suggested, "Write the word *adult* next to their photos in big bold letters, especially when you see them make unwise choices. It's usually better to bite your tongue even if you're crying inside. And pray that they'll ask for your advice."

The most prominent problem voiced in my interviews with seniors was that of making these important relationships with their adult offspring more mutually beneficial. Some expressed a sense of feeling used—always expected to babysit or help with projects or come up with cash. They faced the thorny problem of setting boundaries and occasionally saying no.

In contrast, some folks felt resented and rebuffed. Sharon had done some difficult inner work with a spiritual director in examining her fragile feelings as a mother and grandmother. "I felt ignored and invisible," she said, "and I was always getting my feelings hurt. I finally had to deal with my own ego investment in being needed by my children. The truth was, I needed them to need me, and I wanted them to actually enjoy my company, rather than simply 'do their duty.' It was my responsibility to get a life of my own and allow them to live theirs. But when you genuinely want to be part of their lives and feel patronized, it's hard to let that go." Then she added sadly, "Being tolerated and being loved are two different things. Young folks think we can't tell the difference, but we can."

Which brings me to their valuable advice on when and when not to offer your opinions—even when you feel your wisdom is exactly what they need—and when to let it be. Here is a compilation of their comments:

When to Speak

When You're Asked. Connie learned a surprising lesson about helping her daughter-in-law. Wanting desperately to be helpful on her visits, she would bustle in and tackle laundry, meals, cleaning house—doing chores that ranged from scrubbing bathrooms to moving dishes to the "right" cabinet. Naturally, the daughter-in-law felt inadequate and diminished, even while being grateful for the help.

Connie eventually saw her error and began to offer her assistance with language like, "I have plenty of time today. How can I help you? Would you like me to take the children to the park so you can have some time for yourself? Or would you prefer that I prepare dinner?" Her daughter-in-law had the right to choose how, when, or *if* she wished to be helped—or if she preferred that Connie simply be a guest. (And best not to offer to clean out that cluttered closet.)

It's a good idea to omit decorating ideas, too. Leave the lamp where it is, unless you're asked. Don't reorganize the tools in the garage unless they clearly want you to.

When You Are Affirming. Words of praise are never out of line. It's a challenge to be a responsible adult, and good behavior needs to be encouraged through affirmation—often and with sincerity. Even if you are surrounded by dirty laundry and dust bunnies, it's appropriate to say, "I've noticed how often you read to your toddlers. They're lucky to have you for a mother." Or, to a son or son-in-law, "You seem to genuinely enjoy the company of your wife and children, making time for family outings. You're building great memories with them—I'm proud of you." That familiar old phrase, "Accentuate the positive," is a reliable rule to follow.

When You Offer Support. We assume that our kids know they have our support during tough times, but it often needs to be stated unequivocally. If they've encountered failure or made a mistake, they may feel undeserving of support. But say it once; don't badger them by constant repetition. They probably heard you the first time.

When Not to Speak

When Grandchildren Are Disciplined. Should they spank or not? Should they ground the teenager or not? Unless violence is part of the scenario, button your lip. Studies have shown that as long as children are surrounded with love, many methods of discipline are permissible.

When Couples Are Squabbling. Unless there is physical abuse involved, let them work it out. Many relationships are littered with the rubble of parental intrusion. Offer to take the grandchildren to the movies. Pray for the welfare of the marriage. And don't behave in such a reactive way that they must deal not only with their own distress but with yours as well.

When Babysitting. Unless there's a burning necessity to report bad behavior, use a neutral reply when asked how the grandchildren behaved, such as, "They were just fine." There's no need to give a blow-by-blow report of who did what and who said what, unless there is blood on the floor. Negative reports often make parents feel guilty and responsible for the havoc wreaked by Dennis the Menace while they were away.

Ditto for letting them know how tired you are. Upon their return, saying you're going to take a short nap is different from saying, "They have worn me out, and I'm completely exhausted."

When There's Trouble. Even if your adult children have made a mess of things—financially, spiritually, or parentally— withhold criticism, implied or explicit. Anything that even suggests incompetence or stupidity (even when justified) goes better left unsaid, if you want your relationship with them to survive the storm. Wait for them to ask for your advice.

When the cry for Mom and Dad is no longer part of our daily discourse, we are free to discover the pieces of us that remain, focusing on responsibility for our own behavior. The task is to live out of our best selves, to love as God loves—without expecting anything back. That means no manipulating for certain outcomes and worrying about "What if it doesn't work? What if I don't get the relational result I want?" The truth is that our efforts to "say this so they'll think that" or "do this and they'll do that" are far from a sure thing.

Besides, control is an illusion: *we may have influence, but we don't have control.* Spiritual freedom from our fragile egos comes through doing and saying what is appropriate, valid, and loving, and letting go of the outcome. In doing so, we may discover a deep joy in the process of loving unconditionally.

One of our goals as parents should be to hear our children say someday, "Our parents love us, but their happiness is not dependent on what we do." Perhaps one of the greatest gifts we can give our children is a life of our own, modeling for them a vibrancy in our later years that encourages them in their own aging process. When we allow God to nurture our own inner core and live out of that reservoir of love, we can convey a sense that it's possible to be happy in an uncertain world.

Honoring Memories

I thank my God every time I remember you.
PHILIPPIANS 1:3

Memories of loved ones are like songs in our soul.
MARTHA WAKELEY

"Tell me if I've already told you this," my friend insisted as she began her story. It's a phrase that creeps into casual conversations as we grow older. To be sure, declining memory is the butt of jokes among our peers and derision from the young. We know all too well the panic of flipping through a mental filing cabinet in search of the right word or a familiar name, only to have it pop into our heads two hours later.

Better to laugh than to lament, but why not find ways to honor memory, to cherish it for the gift it is? Though we are familiar with the downside of memory, many seniors are finding ways to emphasize the upside by intentionally sharing their memories with family and friends.

Emotional or Ethical Wills. This kind of will carries no dollar signs; values are bequeathed, not valuables. It is designed as a way for you to share your thoughts, values, lessons in life, passions, hopes, and dreams with your family and friends. You don't want to leave this life with things left unsaid. There are books available in most bookstores as well as online documents that contain prompts and questions to shape your life story and the wisdom you wish to pass on to future generations.

Video and Tape Recordings. Use whatever technology is available to simply speak your remembrances in your own words, adding whatever commentary and advice that comes from your heart.

Photo Scrapbooks. Marian gathered pictures reflecting her life with each child, grandchild, or family unit as a way of honoring their presence in her life. She personalized each collection of photos with messages and memories. "Who knows," she said with a smile, "one fine day, it may find its way into some grandson's treasure chest!"

Trips to Yesteryear. Each spring my sisters and I take our two aunts (now ages eighty-nine and ninety-nine) on an annual "Cemetery Tour" in west Tennessee. With a station wagon brimming with flowers, we visit the graves of dozens of extended family members, decorating the gravesites and tracing the lineage as far back as we can. Sharing stories of saints and rascals under the family tree produces misty eyes, as well as gales of laughter.

Honoring memories has its place in the grieving process also. It's a way of paying tribute to the presence of the lost loved one and focusing on the meaningful intersections of her life with ours. Grief, love, and sometimes even anger can be simultaneously present when we neither idealize nor demonize the person, but remember her just as she was—a human mixture of light and shadow.

The Ritual of the Rose contains significant symbolism as a means of honoring the life of someone who has died. It goes like this: purchase a long-stemmed rose, complete with thorns. Standing beside a lake or river, pull a petal from the rose as you recall each good memory and toss it in the water. When unpleasant or irritating memories arise, pluck a thorn from the stem and throw it in also. As the rose becomes free of all its petals and thorns, toss the whole thing in the water to symbolize your release of that person. It's a beautiful ceremony of letting go that affirms the reality of relationships; they are all a "mixed bag."

Though many excellent texts have been published about the grieving process, there is one vivid metaphor that has stuck with me for years. It is contained in my book *How Can I Let Go If I Don't Know I'm Holding On?* and was suggested by an emergency room physician. He likened an emotional wound to a physical wound, explaining it like this:

> Let's say you come into the ER with a gash in your arm
> that needs stitches.... As a physician, I must tend the

wound, paying careful attention to cleaning out bacteria and probing it for other areas of injury. Only then can I sew it up and allow God's natural healing process to do its remarkable work. Even the scab itself is evidence of automatic healing taking place. I don't make the mistake of taking out the stitches tomorrow to check and see if it is healing properly. You and I must trust the innate process, then accept the scar.[3]

In his view, the pain resulting from a loss must also be tended with care. Only by feeling the sorrow and paying close attention to the emotional wound can we open ourselves to God's healing process. He counseled further, "Beware of the dangers of staying busy and covering up the pain. The grief will just lodge somewhere else, erupting in inappropriate and unhealthy ways—hasty remarriage, physical symptoms, disastrous financial decisions, and other outgrowths of 'Surely I'll feel better if I do this ...'"

The value of honoring memories is beautifully summed up in this poem by Steve Garnaas-Holmes:

> *Bottle up all your life.*
> > *Go ahead: every day, past and future:*
> > *all the great accomplishments and failures,*
> > *the elegant leaps and pratfalls, the love*
> > *you've left behind, the undiscovered miracles,*
> > *the little kindnesses, impossible to measure,*
> > *the things you've said (you've forgotten them),*
> > *words of comfort or wisdom, the lousy jokes,*
> > *the days spent doing chores, letters you wrote*
> > *and didn't write, nights lying awake,*
> > *years spent longing for brilliance,*
> > *moments staring at the sea, acts of courage,*
> > *all the little trips down the sidewalk to the mailbox,*
> > *the people you've touched (don't bother counting,*
> > *you can't even know. Just pour them in)—*

and all that is to come: the speeches and silences,
the gallant deeds and silly stunts,
all of your prayers and their shallowness
and unfathomable grace, your quiet glowing,
how you will grow old, the way you will walk
when you are eighty-five, the things you will say
to those much younger than yourself.
Oh, and your death, your dwindling down,
your last surrendering, and what you leave,
breath seeping out of you like light ...
Take it all and bottle it up and put it on the shelf
And forget it for a long time.
When you remember again, uncork it and see
if that water hasn't been changed to finest wine.
Don't ask me how, but it happens every time. [4]

Beyond the Front Door

"We live our lives in ever-widening circles," reflected Charles, as he extolled the virtues of giving back. "If we don't," he warned, "we risk becoming both bored and boring."

A significant number of older adults expressed this concern. As they talked about the shifts in relationships and circumstances, they cautioned against becoming too self-absorbed in the later years. Marie admitted, "If I don't watch out, it becomes all about me—my aches and pains, my finances, my digestive system, my decline, my death—and the universe stops at the end of my nose. The world shrinks to fit only the existence of *me and mine.*"

When our connections to others get broken, we become broken ourselves. There's a natural compassion for fellow human beings that is severed by self-centeredness. Remember the visceral response when we see a child's finger pricked for a blood test? Our insides contract and we wince in shared pain, do we not? It's an accurate illustration of our proper place in the human family; when one person is injured, we all bleed.

Reach Out to Family

We don't have to save the world. Horace decided to start in his own backyard; he first reached out to family members. "I decided it was time to clean up my part in family squabbles," he reported. "I started getting in touch with those I had neglected or had strained relationships with and mending broken fences before it's too late. I even organized a big reunion at the state park, and cousins came from all directions. We had forgotten there were so many of us! We felt like a family again."

Burt had been a busy business professor all his life and was still full of vigor when he retired. Rather than doing contract work for a business consulting firm, he made a surprising decision to devote all available time and energy toward being a positive part of the lives of his five grandchildren. He babysat often; he took them on trips; he attended ball games and recitals; he spent one-on-one "slow time" with each child to affirm his or her uniqueness. Instead of lavishing gifts on them, he lavished *time*.

"After all," he offered with a smile, "I've discovered how children spell the word *love*. It's T-I-M-E."

Reach Out to Friends

Louise, a single woman whose few family members live far away, reached out beyond her back door by focusing on her friends. "I was tired of hearing myself say (usually at a funeral) 'I meant to visit her last week but I just didn't get around to it.' Or 'I intended to give him a call but watched that old TV movie instead.'"

When we search for ways to reach beyond our small circle, we don't need to span the globe. We can start with acting on our basic intentions, our God-given impulses toward compassion. Put bluntly, if we say we're going to do it, then we need to *do it*. Procrastination is an easy avenue for our laziness and empty intentions.

If we *say* a friendship matters to us, then it's up to us to *act* on it. Ellen has taught me volumes about the power of lived intentions. She's one of those rare people who doesn't pay mere lip service to friendship; she puts legs on it. We lived in the same

Texas neighborhood for little more than a year, but it was enough time to form a bond of friendship that we both valued.

Though each of us has moved several times since our meeting more than twenty years ago, we've managed to keep our connection alive through phone calls, letters, e-mails, and an unbelievable number of locations—from Miami to New Mexico and points in between—where we have met for what we call "forty-eight-hour marathons." Our friendship has become such a priority for us that we no longer say *whether*, but *when* and *where*.

Reach Out to the World

"I can't save the world," said Joan, "but I can join with others in making a difference. Together, we can build hospitals, support the arts, and feed flood victims." Alone, we often feel helpless to alleviate the overwhelming suffering of our brothers and sisters around the globe, but together we can move mountains. The spiritually healthy person tends to the health of others.

Many organizations have proven track records for both effectiveness and financial fitness. Not only did Joan check them out, then write a check, but she volunteered locally to counsel the homeless at the Hub, a haven in downtown Memphis for those who need help rather than a handout. Her generous heart and determination to extend the boundaries of her world reflect an inner vigor that keeps her young inside.

Murray provided care for a child in Cambodia for a few dollars a month through an international organization. Sarah tutors in math and English at an underfunded school. Martha inspired a group at her church to "adopt" a local school. Together and separately, we can put flesh and bone on the benevolent grace of God. We can find surprising joy in doing unreturnable favors and unrewarded tasks.

Reaching out also includes addressing the primary causes of the world's distress by involvement in peace and justice issues. Claire decided to put her passion for social justice to work by volunteering for an organization called Bread for the World, while

Henry used his carpentry skills to build houses for Habitat for Humanity. Many organizations devoted to changing social policy depend on the energy and commitment of the elderly to give voice and vigor to worthwhile causes.

I noticed something significant in those seniors who made a concerted effort to reach out to others. They used less "us-and-them" language, as if they no longer needed an enemy to rail against. Their sense of separation dissolved. Their sense of their own problems diminished. They began to build bridges instead of borders. They moved from hubris to humanity, from isolation to involvement.

As you develop a more genuine connection to the soul and the divine values embedded there, you find clarity about what really matters. With little to stand in the way, love of family, friends, and the world can deepen. Tears may come more easily. Expressions of gratitude and affection may be spoken from lips that once guarded them.

Moreover, there's a surprising paradox that emerges for those with ears to hear and hearts to understand: a desire for both solitude and community. While the bonds of relationships may strengthen, there is a growing sense of ultimate aloneness—not in a desperate way, but in a realistic way. It becomes clear that no one except God accompanies us through the common experiences of birth and death. Though we share that with all sentient beings, each of us makes those journeys without human companions. We are connected to each other with bonds of family, friends, and community, yet we are alone.

Marie reflected this realization in her answer to the question about what she wanted to experience as she aged. "I want to be part of a community with shared values," she said. "Yet at the same time, I want to nurture my sense of who I am individually in relationship to God."

Writer Parker Palmer expressed it clearly in *A Hidden Wholeness*:

If we are to hold solitude and community together as a true paradox, we need to deepen our understanding of both poles. *Solitude* does not necessarily mean living apart from others; rather, it means never living apart from one's self. It is not about the absence of other people—it is about being fully present to ourselves, whether or not we are with others. *Community* does not necessarily mean living face-to-face with others; rather, it means never losing the awareness that we are connected to each other. It is not about the presence of other people—it is about being fully open to the reality of relationship, whether or not we are alone.[5]

Relationships are messy, even in later life. But, seen through the lens of a lifetime, they become more precious than gold. Maybe with the wisdom of years, we become capable of focusing on our love for one person, while at the same time wrapping our arms around the world.

Looking Inside

1. How has your view of friendship changed during later years? Has your measuring stick remained the same?

2. How do you maintain the friendships that you value?

3. Review your relationship history. How would you reflect on your times of renegotiation?

4. What methods of honoring lost loved ones have been most meaningful to you? How would you like to be honored or remembered after your death?

5. In what ways are you currently reaching out to others—family, friends, the world? How might you strengthen those connections?

5

Surprises of the Sacred

Our souls are restless till they find their rest in Thee.
ST. AUGUSTINE

I've spent my whole life sitting in a pew learning about God and working in the church trying to please God," Gwen reflected. "Now I want something deeper. I feel as if I've been behaving well and working for someone I've read about and heard about, but have never actually met. You might say that I've read the Boss's memos, obeyed the directives, and gotten some things accomplished in His 'business,' but I've always assumed He was holed up in that lofty heavenly office of His. Now I want Him to move in with me, bag and baggage!" Gwen was yearning to move from thinking about God to experiencing God. It appeared that belief and knowledge alone have limited value. As popular humorist Garrison Keillor has quipped on *Prairie Home Companion,* "Sitting in church doesn't make you a Christian any more than standing in your garage makes you a car!"

When I asked seniors about their relationship with the sacred, their responses were full of yet more surprises. Their comments ran the gamut from abandonment of religion to reconnection to religion, from rejection of familiar creeds to seeing them

93

with new eyes. Some insisted they had lost their faith; many said they had found it. In almost all cases, the issues of later life forced them to honestly confront their beliefs and behaviors. One senior expressed it this way: "When death is right around the corner, denial no longer works very well."

Eighty-five-year-old Darrell illustrated this struggle. "I finally had the guts to ask myself if I really believed this stuff or if I had just attended church to rub shoulders with my friends and be a good example to the kids. But I can assure you that it was a little unsettling to ask myself those questions."

In the realm of the sacred, I discovered that seniors were examining everything from the particulars of prayer to aspects of the afterlife. Stanley summed it up like this: "There's a qualitative difference between believing with the head and believing with the heart. I'm no longer willing to accept inadequate answers just so I can have one."

Men and women in later life long to experience the Holy as the cement that holds their lives together, instead of merely window dressing.

God and Me

"My image of God started spilling over the edges of any 'container' I put it in," explained Carrie. "I went from seeing God as a distant, demanding Father to companionable Friend to nurturing Mother to powerful Creator ... and now? Now God seems so big that I can't find enough names ... Comforter, Redeemer, Prince of Peace, Source of All.... Every name I can think of is inadequate. It's both 'all of the above' and 'none of the above.'"

Anthony described his journey this way: "I started out like most everyone else—thinking of God as righteous judge (white male, of course), proclaiming that if I said and did the right things, I would have a one-way ticket to heaven. Then I realized how self-centered my motives were. Underneath my faith was the unspoken desire to get something out of the deal—heaven, peace of mind, good reputation, whatever. I want to move from what I can *get* from God to what I can *give*."

Walter's image was undergoing renovation also. "For me, God is no longer that judgmental old geezer who selectively answers prayers or coldly rejects them, but an immanent, transcendent Creator of the universe and all that is. I think it's possible to fall in love with that Mystery."

Diane found that her relationship with God deepened through creativity. "When I started painting in my later years, my image of God exploded. It seemed like a sacred movable feast, something that couldn't be caught or contained, but was everywhere I looked—in the smile of a child, the elegance of an eagle, the blinding yellow of tulips, the smell of yeasty bread, the eyes of my husband—everything seemed infused with the Holy. It's just like Elizabeth Barrett Browning said it was: earth is truly 'crammed with heaven.'"

Some found this movement from a humanlike entity to a more mysterious Presence unsettling. "I didn't know what to hold on to," Susie said. "It was scary to think of God as a formless Spirit. I wanted to know Someone loved and cared about *me personally*. I had been trying to figure out all this stuff about the Trinity (it had always confused me), when I had a dream that gave me incredible peace. Want to hear it? I hope you won't think it's silly!"

> In the dream, a kind of ineffable Presence came to me—very gently—and told me not to worry about it, to 'lighten up!' Then there were these words: Here's how it is, Susie—God the Creator is a powerful *formless* force of energy that infuses everything, that gives Life to life. God the Son is this loving force in *form* (Jesus in your tradition) so that you can see what that Love looks like in a human being. The Holy Spirit is *wisdom*, the ongoing guidance that is available inside you, moment to moment.[1]

It didn't seem silly to me. The dream gave Susie an expanded view of God that was clearly providing ongoing meaning to her life, and through her sharing, to all of us as well.

Matthew's experience of the Holy felt intensely personal. As he grew older and dealt with the loss of his wife to Alzheimer's, he felt as if Jesus walked and talked with him, comforting and strengthening him. "I feel closer to God than I ever have in my life," he said with a confident smile, "and Jesus sticks with me like a brother."

Quite a number were less sure in their later years of exactly who God is and were becoming comfortable with the mysterious uncertainty. Ed offered, "My experiences in life have made me realize that the realm of the Sacred—God, if you will—is more a reality to live into than a puzzle to be solved. Even in spite of all the evidence to the contrary, I still believe there's a basic benevolence at the heart of things ... that Somebody up there, out there, in here, really loves us. I'm not sure what It is, and I can't prove Its existence, but I believe we can trust It."

In some instances, the search for the sacred led to a storehouse of buried doubts. "The problem of suffering makes me doubt the love and mercy of God," admitted a former pastor. "I want a sign to confirm the benevolence of God and explain why the universe is not more friendly."

A contrasting viewpoint came from Louise, who offered this metaphor: "I've come to see life not as a brutal cosmic 'boot camp,' but a school of the soul that refines and reveals our true Selves. Of course, we never graduate from that school, do we?"

Jim spoke of his relationship in terms of freedom. "I have a more authentic connection to God than I used to," he explained, "ever since I realized that I don't have to compromise who I really am or make myself a clone of someone else. I feel I'm loved and forgiven—warts and all. Being good does not rule out being real; the two are not incompatible."

Jim had run out of steam in trying to find an image of God that was satisfying. "Certainly, it isn't visual," he insisted. "I can't even say it's a creative force. To me, any words turn out to be inadequate, and that's somehow a great comfort to me. No math theorem, no proof, no intellectual answer—so it has to be something bigger that was before me, after me, a part of me, a part of the grand whole. Frankly, I'm finished wrestling with it."

Matthew talked about his realization of the "kingdom within." "I no longer think of God as something *outside* me or someone who is judging what I do. When Jesus says that 'God makes His home in us,' I get a taste of mystery—the kingdom within that the Bible mentions so often. After all, I'm made in the image of God ... so doesn't that mean that at least a spark of God resides inside me?"

The description of the Holy that was given most often, however, was that of Light—not personal, but pervasive; not a Being, but Being itself; that which animates everything from plants to human beings. And I was surprised to discover that even though thoughts of death were unavoidable, many seniors possessed an underlying trust that diffused their anxiety with faith.

Somewhere along the journey of these interviews, I noticed other aspects of the changing images of God, patterns underneath the varied descriptions I heard. There seemed to be a mysterious corollary between a deepening knowledge of yourself and a more expansive image of God—that is, the increased connection with the soul sparked an increased connection with the One who infuses the soul. Something else, Someone else, lives there, too, a Presence greater, wiser, braver, and more loving than our own limited selves. That divine voice knocks at the door of the heart, whispering insights and challenges, and nudging us toward the good, helping us become closer to our true selves in relationship with that Presence.

That ever-enlarging image of God keeps spilling over the edges of any container we put it in or any definition we concoct. The results of that awareness are striking: an increasing sense of partnership, a responsibility for participation in the divine process of growth, a feeling of friendship with God, rather than domination by God, and a need to serve the community.

When your image of God expands, God becomes more than a sovereign to be feared and obeyed. Those who saw God only as a kind of all-powerful ruler, capable of making anything happen with the wink of the divine eye, tended to be fearful, judgmental, and subservient. They saw their lives as dependent on God to do everything for them, resulting in an immature relationship with someone they were afraid of, as if they were helpless in the face of God's powerful will.

On the other hand, those who imagined the power of God in an atmosphere of wonder had a firmer grip on the reality of free will—the startling sense of responsibility for our own gift of participation in our own lives and the life of the world. We always have a choice in how we respond to this challenge, even when it appears that everything is determined for us.

When all is said and done, it may be that the deeper function of faith is not to turn our anxiety into answers, but to turn our anxiety into awe.

Rethinking Prayer

In their important book *Primary Speech*, writers Ann and Barry Ulanov remind us that we were born to pray. In delight and euphoria, a natural impulse to say "thank you" erupts from deep inside us. When we encounter trouble and trauma, we instinctively call out for help. Consider every culture and you see the evidence: whirling dervishes whirl, rain dancers dance, penitents bow. In conversations about their relationship with the sacred dimension of their lives, many seniors shared both the struggle and the strength they found in the practice of prayer.

"I don't expect as much from God as I used to," said Karen. "I've stopped thinking of God as my personal butler, granting my wishes if I begged hard enough and behaved well enough. That seems arrogant to me now.... Prayer has to be more than that. Besides, doesn't constant pleading show a lack of trust?"

Richard spoke of the inherent nature of his trust when he offered, "I don't even pray for God to be *with me* anymore, because that seems to be a *given*.... God is always with us. I pray to be aware and open to that divine Presence, no matter how things turn out. After all, even Jesus didn't always get his way. When he prayed in the garden of Gethsemane to 'remove this cup from me' (Luke 22:42), he was crucified anyway. But God was with him every step of the way, even to the cross. My prayers these days seem to be less about God changing things to suit me and more about God changing me so that I can be the channel of love that I was meant to be, no matter what happens."

Prayer is more about relationship than results. A great many of us in later life seem to be moving toward that same conclusion. When Edgar was diagnosed with a life-threatening heart condition, he reflected, "I had some mixed reactions when all those people were praying for my survival. Though I was genuinely grateful for their prayers, it was their loving support that warmed my heart the most. The practical part of me kept saying, 'If everyone lived that was prayed for on our planet, it would be terribly overpopulated!' I finally quit trying to figure it all out. When people love you enough to pray for you, it's the love that matters."

One of the most thoughtful comments about the nature of prayer came from Betty, a feisty, energetic seventy-two-year-old woman with a debilitating eye ailment. "I had been healthy all my life and certainly wasn't accustomed to defeat and discouragement," she insisted. "But when my condition failed to improve, I was at a crossroads—a crisis of faith, I guess. I made a decision to move from stomping my feet to an attitude of acceptance. Believe me, it was a big step and a tough one."

Betty also began to rethink her theology of prayer. "When folks gave me assurances that 'God is in charge; just put yourself in God's hands and God will restore your sight,' I had to wrestle with the negative results I was experiencing. Was I not good enough? Did I need to double the number in the prayer group? I knew these caring friends meant well, but I kept asking myself why God would heal me and not some suffering child in Darfur who was also being prayed for. It was so confusing ... it made God sound capricious and arbitrary, and I knew that wasn't the nature of the God I had worshiped all my life."

As she moved from protest and pleading to acceptance and trust, she focused on doing her part in the process, cooperating with medical instructions and doing the activities she could still do with grace and gratitude. "I chose to maintain my faith in the loving nature of God, even though it was a mystery to me. After all, I couldn't believe God was a magician doing random tricks or a celestial servant ready to do my bidding, so I let go of the results and nurtured the relationship instead."

Though it can be difficult to describe your prayer life, a significant number of respondents seemed to be moving from more structured personal prayer to more contemplative, wordless experiences, realizing that many things could be considered prayer. If prayer is viewed broadly as "loving attention to God" or "the pilgrimage from the soul to the sacred," then anything that draws us closer to that divinity is in the realm of prayer—hearing inspiring music, standing before a beautiful painting, watching an eagle soar, running a marathon, rocking a child, listening to words that stir our spirits—the possibilities are endless. Mindful experiences such as these move us toward the habit of humble listening; they close our mouths and open our ears. As one clever senior put it, "Have you ever wondered why we were given two ears and only one mouth?"

None of us can adequately explain the many paradoxes of prayer. But I believe we can trust that the One who created our deep instinct to pray somehow hears those prayers ... and that we ourselves are shaped by the praying. Maybe it's more about joining in the *Spirit's prayers for us and all creation* than manipulating divine energy. Prayer is a way we honor something greater, something infinitely more loving than we can imagine, a divine benevolence at the heart of things. I, along with many others in later life, pray to be a part of that loving energy.

Charlie's cryptic comment on the subject of prayer was brief and direct. With a shrug of his broad shoulders, he said, "The only prayer that makes sense to me anymore is *'Thank you.'*"

Heaven, Hell, or Something Else

"When we die, I think our souls will move into close association with other souls in some kind of unusual understanding, but I no longer have to know the details of what that will look like," Stanley said tentatively. "Frankly, the process seems like a continuum.... We're born, we die, then there's something else—a *doorway*, not a brick wall. I think we retain an identity of sorts, but it will be a different kind."

Stanley's opinion about the afterlife was one of scores of thoughtful answers that ran the gamut from skepticism to security. Some expressed their thoughts in concept; some used metaphors. A majority of those interviewed seemed to exhibit less interest in the particulars of the afterlife than they were in the realities of this life. They were less afraid of dying than they were of living in a helpless, painful state of existence with little quality of life.

This was further reflected in Martha's comments: "My concept of the afterlife has changed dramatically since I was young. Having been raised a Baptist on the traditional 'plan of salvation,' I was pretty focused on going to heaven. Now that those beliefs have been replaced, I'm skeptical, but open. Because the human mind is naturally tuned to justice issues, I think that some mechanism for equalizing the inequities of this earth might be a fair thing, but I'm still unsure. Anyway, I think faith is not about what happens when we die; it's about how we live."

Raymond agreed. "I'm not focused on what happens to me after I die. I just want to live life fully so I can contribute toward a tipping point of spiritual evolution on this planet. The important question for me is, 'How well have I learned to *love?*'"

Several people had found strength as they witnessed death firsthand. Sue spoke of her mother's final moments. "It was evident to me that her spirit left her body," she remembered. "She was no longer really in that room, and the atmosphere was peaceful and loving and full of light. It was such a comfort to me."

One of the most dramatic end-of-life events was described by Lawrence, an eighty-five-year-old aristocratic gentleman who had retired from his successful business. When I asked him if there was anything about growing older that he hadn't told anyone, he hesitated for several silent minutes. Then, choking back tears, he spoke of a numinous experience in the hospital room of a dying friend that he had been reluctant to share. "As the Episcopal priest read the healing ritual," he recalled, "I sensed—no, I *saw*— the Holy Spirit at the side of the bed. At that moment, all that I had thought of as empty ritual—creeds that had been meaning-less—became real to me. I haven't been the same since," he mum-bled, "and all my fear is gone. It was an incredible experience."

Herbert's faith was strengthened by his own near-death experiences. "During my heart attack, I died and was resuscitated six times," he reported. "Each time, I had a keen awareness of other aspects of reality, and when I returned to my body, all I could feel was profound peace and joy and compassion."

The diverse concepts of the afterlife reflected the unique-ness and life experiences of the interviewees. Their comments were shaped by education, beliefs, personality, and events. Here are more examples:

- It feels like going home, as if the Divine Spark within me—my soul—is going back to where it came from.
- I think it's a continuation of growth; to me, not to grow or develop would be pure hell.
- I doubt if there's an afterlife; I think we live on in our children and grandchildren.
- I hope it's an unfolding of Truth, a revelation of sorts. I'm looking forward to that.
- It's more superstition than reality—a control mecha-nism to keep us in line. We shouldn't have to be rewarded for living with integrity; goodness is its own reward.
- To send one group to heaven and the other to hell doesn't jibe with the nature of God that Jesus revealed. Jesus was loving, accepting, nonviolent,

irrationally forgiving. Personally, I think *God* is the one who forgives seventy times seven!

- The jury is out on this afterlife business, and I don't think we should be trying to figure it out. If we spent our time following the example of Jesus to love God and love others, trying to do that would fill up our plates.

- Heaven and hell are not necessarily later; we create them right here on this earth.

A few older adults chose to express their impressions of the afterlife in metaphor and story. Here is Keith's description: "I think it's a situation where I'm on one side of a filmy purple curtain," he mused. "Death is the breeze that billows the curtain and finally takes it away."

Bart's colorful comments provide a fitting conclusion to the discussion of this great mystery. He decided to hang his hat on a traditional biblical parable (laced with his clever sense of humor) that gave him hope in the nature of the afterlife. "Are there streets of gold? Or is death a series of misfirings in the brain that cause weird images? I don't know. I no longer worry *if* or *what*. It's the *who* part that gives me confidence. Remember the story of the loving father and the prodigal son? The father greets his bad boy with open arms and loving acceptance and crazy forgiveness and says plain as day, 'I'm throwing you a big party—the fatted calf and music and all the trimmings. Just come to the party with me and your brother!' So I don't need to know any of the details or what orchestra is playing."

Hearing the Spirit's Guidance

> *Let anyone who has an ear listen to what the Spirit is saying.*
> REVELATION 2:7

Standing in the middle of the cluttered room, Barry surveyed box after box of office items. He had recently called it quits at the university and eagerly moved to a cozy farmhouse with his wife, Ruth. Their retirement dream was right there in the middle of ten green acres—barn and all.

Mixed with the excitement, however, was an unsettled feeling—a what-next restlessness. The apprehension was even finding its way into daily decisions, such as, "What shall I hang on my new office walls?" As he prepared to nail up his impressive collection of diplomas and awards, he stopped the hammer in midair. Something didn't seem to fit. A nagging question popped into his mind: "Does this really represent who I am at this point in my life?" He put down the hammer and poured a cup of coffee.

"It took me quite a long time to get that hammer out again," Barry confided. "I decided to take my own sweet time and see which items in the box reflected my values now. You'll never guess what I finally hung—a picture of my new horse, a doodle painting from one of the grandchildren, a framed poem that I cherish, and a group photo of the whole extended family. Those things felt congruent with what was real inside my soul, my deepest values. It just seemed 'right.'"

So what did Barry hear with his inner voice? What does it mean when something "feels right"? How did he distinguish between the voice of the soul where the Divine meets us and all the other voices inside? Most of us have heard the usual pat answers:

- The wisdom you need is all inside you.
- Just obey the scriptures and everything will be revealed to you.
- Don't worry; the Holy Spirit will guide you.
- All you have to do is be *yourself*!

Sadly, we know lots about what we *ought* to do and precious little about *how* to do it. Listening merely takes time and focus; truly *hearing* is another matter. It takes genuine openness and vulnerability to wisdom that is not necessarily our own.

As we saw in chapter 3, the body delivers some of these messages to us if we learn to heed its language. Hearing God speak through our souls, however, involves a more subtle set of signals. Those spiritual nudges usually come in a whisper, not a shout—in a nudge, not a shove. To become familiar with this remarkable inner landscape where the Holy guides us, we must carefully travel its mystical terrain and learn its contours. We also need to know where the land mines are.

Most of us do this inner work with fear and trembling—and rightly so. Max voiced his suspicion of one of the emotional land mines he repeatedly encountered: the desire for absolute certainty. "I spent most of my life trying to be right, the one with the answers. Slowly I realized that my desire to be right was sabotaging my relationships, my growth, and my peace of mind. It kept me stuck and arrogant. Now, it makes me uneasy when folks say, 'God told me …' Isn't it more accurate to say, 'It occurred to me …'? After all, people have done some pretty horrible things through the years under the guise of 'the Lord wants me to.' I guess all of us have a tendency to hear the voice of our own ego and call it good or even call it God."

Writer and theologian Robert Morris suggested that this desire for certainty could well be dubbed the eighth deadly sin and can be a hindrance to realistic wisdom. In an article in the spiritual journal *Weavings*, he wrote:

> Active faith, a living trust in God's ability to lead and guide, most always involves … an edge of uncertainty … that is, enough certainty to set out may be all we get. And why should we expect something manifestly supernatural? God works through our reason as we hear Scripture and apply it to our world. God works through our care and concern as we pray for others and reach out in works of compassion and justice. God works through our love to touch the hearts of others with divine love. Why wouldn't God work through our innate, natural capacities for

imagination and intuition to communicate?... Depth psychology observes that all human beings seem to have a built-in ... guidance system that speaks through hunch and dream, aha's and epiphanies.[2]

When speaker Marjorie Thompson, author of *Soul Feast*, was teaching at the Tennessee Academy for Spiritual Formation, she said the same thing in these memorable words: "Doubt scrapes the barnacles off the ship of faith."[3] She made a significant distinction between different kinds of doubt, however. She spoke of negative doubt as fear-based and resistant, while positive doubt invites us to inquiry, curiosity, and a search for truth. This approach to discernment encourages us to put our opinions and decisions through a special spiritual filter, a way of testing the value of our inner promptings.

Consider questions such as these:

- Will this outcome produce fear or joy?
- What will be the fruit of this way of thinking or acting?
- Does it promote the pathway of Love?
- Does it enlarge or diminish me or others?

Howard's interview underscored this desire to make sound decisions in this last part of life, but revealed yet another conundrum. "The trouble is, my decisions are not usually between good and bad; they're more likely to be between better and best. Lately, my wife and I have been feeling fenced in by all the wonderful things we have. We enjoy all these fruits of our labor, but we don't want to spend the rest of our lives taking care of our *stuff*. Should we sell the house and move to a smaller one? Should we move to the city where the kids live? Should we skip that intermediate step and go straight to a retirement community? Fay and I are faithful churchgoers and we would like to pray about this, but we don't quite know how."

Though most of us in this generation were taught *not* to trust our feelings, there is a growing appreciation for the powerful channel of divine guidance provided by our emotional system. Howard and Fay were encouraged to get in touch with their "gut reactions" as they entered the discernment process. They imagined themselves moving to different locations and paid attention to the responses of their inner beings. Did they feel relief, excitement, constriction, possibility? As they visited a variety of venues, they listened for internal cues, building deeper trust in divine guidance. Then they had the courage to pray this discernment prayer over a period of time:

> Loving and caring God, if this is the best course of action, if this is what is best for me to do, I pray that you will *increase* the desire within me to do it; but if this is not for the highest good of all concerned, I pray that you will *decrease* the desire within me to do it.

To build trust in this kind of guidance requires a deepening of our relationship with God, a growing familiarity with the sacred dimension of our lives, and a willingness to watch and pray, watch and pray.

Motives and Methods

"I'm a little weary of talking about connection to the Holy and buying more books about it," complained Connie. "I need some tools—some bridges that will help me move from the concept of connection to the actual practice of it."

The conversation with Connie was typical of many responses of those in later life. There was regret about skimming the surface or living in the shadows of a so-so spiritual life. Many felt they had been digging shallow holes in too many places, rather than digging deeply enough to find the living water.

"I used to think of my life as a boat bobbing on top of the water," Connie continued. "That boat gets tossed about by the wind, blowing it this way and that. Sometimes there's a big storm in my life and that boat takes a beating. But it holds because it's anchored in something solid and sure—my faith in God—and that sustains me through the storm."

Then the spiritual surprise came. "So that has been my rationale for the spiritual practices and disciplines I've done all my life. I wanted to maintain that anchor so it would be there when I needed it," she reasoned. "But now that I'm older, I'm seeing things more clearly—more clearly than I want to, actually. I realize that much of my spiritual life has been mostly about *me*—not God, not other people.

"You asked me what I've learned about myself as I've aged, and it's a case of good news and bad news. The good news is that I'm stronger than I thought I was. The bad news is that I'm much more self-serving than I ever dreamed. I've been tending that 'anchor' I mentioned so it would serve me well, keep me steady in the storm. Can't we tend our connection to God out of love, rather than a desire to get something for ourselves?"

She paused to collect her conclusions. "I'm beginning to realize that the ultimate connection with the sacred is loving God for God's sake, not my own; feeling an authentic zest for life even when it isn't zesty; a kind of aliveness that reaches out to others— not for what I can get, but for what I can give. Maybe that's what growth is all about—the more deeply we know God, the more deeply we come to know ourselves, and vice versa. Even at our best, we have mixed motives, don't we? We can't help it—we're human beings, after all. But being aware of our motives helps us move beyond them—and it sure keeps us humble!"

Maintaining that connection—tending that anchor, if you will—is not a one-size-fits-all technique. Bookshelves are bulging with devotional guides and inspirational texts that can serve as "portable pastors," helping us expand our view of all that can nurture our sense of the sacred.

Reading about it, however, is not the same as doing it—a realization expressed by a number of interviewees. "I've understood the concept of the Presence of God all my life," commented Yvonne. "I've just never taken the time and focus to integrate it into my days. Faith seems pretty empty unless it finds its way into the way I live moment to moment."

As I mentioned previously, many in later life realized that nature and creativity opened them to God just as powerfully as scripture and church attendance did. Some found their daily walks contained holy moments. Others found the spiritual components in gardening, cooking, making pottery, cabinet making, meditation, exercise, journaling, or service to others. When choosing your own "connectors," the seniors I spoke with gave these general suggestions:

- Choose a practice that suits you and that you can look forward to.
- Whatever it is, do it daily—not "when you have time."
- Create a special place—an altar, a chair by the window, a bench in the garden—some spot that feels sacred.
- Keep it alive; if a particular practice or devotional book begins to get stale, change it up—there are unlimited resources out there. Let the Spirit lead you to something new.
- Experiment with different methods of prayer; be willing to expand your awareness of the depth and breadth of prayer.[4]
- Befriend the silence; experience it as the "language of God." Practice ways to *still your mind*, and the silence will shape you. Gaining a comfort level with silence involves letting go of filling it with your own thoughts and expectations and trusting that God's transforming grace is at work, even without your micromanagement.[5]
- Slow down to the pace of guidance—that is, live one moment at a time. Don't miss your life while you hurry on to the next thing.

- Find ways to put "legs" on your beliefs and practices. If they aren't transformed into action, they're just hollow words.
- Remember there's no such thing as an idle thought; the mind "eats" just as the body does, and what we give attention to expands into experience.
- *Pay attention;* notice, notice, notice. It leads to gratitude, compassion, and love.

The truth is that almost anything can be done with spiritual awareness, if we cultivate that sensibility. Whether we are simply watching a sunset, singing in a choir, or crying with a friend, everything contains elements of the Holy.

Trusting the Mystery

"You can think things to death," offered Clyde. "I don't have my head in the sand—I know there's meanness in the world—but I also see the unexpected explosions of grace all around me." He went on to mention everyday examples, such as a stranger who jumps in the river to save a drowning child, a fireman who rushes into a burning building to drag a dog to safety, or someone who simply comes up beside your stalled car and offers his jumper cables.

The paradox of the simultaneous presence of both good and evil is a tough pill to swallow for all of us. The older adults I interviewed, however, seemed to have reached a calm level of acceptance in the face of this conundrum. They had moved from trying to figure it all out to accepting the mystery of it.

"I would prefer to make my peace with the uncertainties of life than to concoct an answer just so I'll feel more intellectually satisfied," said Sam. "Being more open to God is not about finding the right answers; it's about having the courage to ask the right questions—What am I here for? How can I love better? Who or what is God? How can I make the world more just? Those important questions shape us ... but at some point, it becomes a leap of radical trust. Or, as Einstein asked, 'Is the universe a friendly place or not?'"

There are plenty of reasons to answer No to that loaded question. Man's inhumanity to man is well documented. In spite of that, the witness of wisdom through the ages comes down on the side of Yes. To answer Yes changes the way we view life and the way we live it. Something harmonious happens when we lean into that affirmation with heart, soul, and mind. Science is telling us that our cells actually change structure, the immune system is strengthened, relationships deepen, and irrational joy and peace emerge. It isn't only our bodies that respond to that divine harmony. We see it all around us in the creative ordering of the universe—the tides, the rotation of the planets, and the structure of atoms.

If the seniors I interviewed are typical, another paradox becomes evident. In some striking way, as your faith becomes more solid, it simultaneously becomes more porous. There is a willingness to examine holes in creeds and theories, to be open to new discoveries, and to make room for puzzlement and paradox.

Even though the divine Mystery at the heart of things can't be totally understood, it can be trusted. And, when taken seriously, it finds its way into the heartbeat of our lives and moves us into the world with compassion.

Looking Inside

1. How would you describe your current relationship to God? Has it changed as you've grown older?

2. What is your earliest memory of prayer? Review the usual ways you have prayed in the past. What about now?

3. How do you hear or sense the Presence of God most keenly? What spiritual practice would you be interested in embracing?

4. When was the last time you experienced a stirring in your soul, a glimpse of the eternal, or a sense of *something more*? What were the circumstances of that epiphany?

Surprising
Challenges

We cannot live the afternoon of life according to the program of life's morning; for what was great in the morning will be little at evening, and what in morning was true will at evening have become a lie.

CARL JUNG

"These later years of my life have thrown down a gauntlet of challenges," Serena offered. "Thank goodness, they mostly appear one at a time, or I might not be able to absorb them all."

Ted spoke of it as a time of trading old trials for new ones. "I've gone from focusing on educating the kids to managing my retirement income, from caring for babies to caring for the physical needs of ailing parents and friends—even my wife and myself. Sometimes it feels as if I've swapped one set of limitations for another."

From sleeping alone to giving up the car, from the decline of the body to the loss of loved ones, from getting a good night's rest to filling empty hours, the array of late-life challenges can be daunting. "If I've learned one thing about this stage of my life, it's this," added Ted. "Lamenting what used to be can sure sap my energy for dealing with what is. I don't want to merely *survive* through these years; I want to *thrive*, if I possibly can."

When I posed the question "What has been your greatest challenge in the aging process?" I was met with such a range of responses that I hardly knew how to catalog them. Some were simple things, such as standing up straight or gripping the pickle jar. Some were more complex, like dealing with a new cell phone or keeping anxiety at bay. Some seniors were trying to manage dwindling incomes; some were having difficulty coming to terms with the life they had lived. Regrets and remembrances, failures and successes, tragedies and triumphs—all were part of the knotty tapestry of a life lived. Some challenges, however, were pointed out much more often than others.

Learning to Fly Solo

The test of living alone won the contest, hands down.

"It's not that I'm helpless," insisted Margie, a recent widow. "But Henry took care of certain things, you know— like changing the oil in the car or getting the roof repaired— and lots more stuff that I took for granted. I've managed to learn about insurance coverage and manage the money details, but I can't seem to make my peace with the loneliness. Most days, that stretch of time from five to ten every evening seems endless."

"My world seems to be shrinking," observed William. "It isn't easy to form new relationships at this age, and I find myself withdrawing more and more. Men seem to have more trouble with this than women do."

Many seniors worried that their families worried. "I don't want to be a burden to my children, but I'm afraid I am. They don't think I can make it on my own, and sometimes I wonder if they're right," said Gordon. "They want me to move to New York near their home, but I don't want to pull up my roots. I'd rather paddle my own canoe right here where I am, but I'm not sure I know how. After all, Denise and I were married for fifty-five years, and being without her feels as if I'm starting over."

Marianne took a proactive approach by intentionally reaching out. "I still love gardening and am physically able to do simple tasks, so I joined the volunteer group at the local botanical gardens. Getting acquainted with other gardeners and pooling our efforts for the good of the community have given me a wonderful boost—and new friends, as well."

Even those who filled their lives with a whirl of daytime activity, however, had to return to an empty house at the close of the day. "Heaven forbid that I should turn into one of those old codgers who depend on the TV for company," protested Philip. "I'm working on turning into my own best friend, plus attempting to make new ones, but I can tell you it's quite a challenge for an introvert like me."

Friends who shared their struggles with loneliness presented a treasure of surprises and suggestions for our consideration. "Whoever said that 'the best cure for loneliness is solitude' was on to something," Annette offered. "It amounts to understanding the difference between being alone and being lonely. When I was first living by myself, I assumed the only cure was to fill the empty space with people, activity, and noise, and I suppose there's nothing wrong with that solution in the short term. But I found I could still be lonely even in a crowd. I had to go to the source of my loneliness, which meant exploring my relationship with myself and with God."

Annette continued with her astute observations. "I discovered that even though solitude and loneliness are both experiences of being alone, I had to sink into solitude willingly if I was going to make any progress. Once I did, it seemed that most of my conversation was taking place in a sort of interior 'chat room' where I talked to myself. I hope you don't think I'm a nutcase, but believe it or not, something or Someone eventually starts to 'talk back'—questioning, analyzing, encouraging, chastising, planning, dreaming. Now when I have one of those desperate spells of whining, that Someone puts her hand on my shoulder and says sternly and compassionately, 'Annette, get a grip, honey. There, there—you're going to be okay ... just hang in there.'"

Others spoke of similar experiences. "When we're engaged in interior dialogue, we are in the good company of ourselves," said Mary with a knowing smile. "To be our own friend means that we curb the inner criticism and give support instead. We can even be a fun-loving companion to ourselves!"

Writer Sue Monk Kidd described it in these eloquent words in her book *Firstlight*: "Solitude becomes a descent into the labyrinths of self, where we set up a dialogue with our own depths."[1] The courage to choose time apart from others and develop the capacity to be alone eventually has healing effects on the mind and spirit. Or, in the wise words of my friend Wayne, "If you don't come apart, you'll come apart."

Those with vivid imaginations described these inner characters as colorful caricatures. "There is a whole host of 'me's' in my inner sanctum," laughed Victoria. "There's the moral self, the critical self, the creative self, the reflective self, the playful self, the lazy self—and that's just for openers. Of course, my awareness of them comes and goes, but I've found that I don't get to know them at all if I run away somewhere."

These escape destinations were pictured as an array of busy distractions—one more project, one more TV show, one more trip to see the grandkids, one more needless trip to the mall.

"I got introduced to my inner self through random, stream-of-consciousness journaling," said Theo, a writer. "Once I got rid of that pesky editor in my head and started writing straight from the heart, those voices inside me began to ramble and rage, to instruct and inspire. Plus, they gave me a growing sense that God was meeting me in that sacred soul space."

Most agreed, however, that it's a matter of choosing to focus on the upside of living alone rather than the downside (which normally grabs the lion's share of attention). Seniors admitted (some grudgingly) that there were some surprising pluses about flying solo:

- Eating what you want when you want to
- Listening to the music you really like and turning up the volume
- Having a choice between cuddling up with a good book or mingling with the concert crowd
- Turning on the light at 2 a.m. and watching an old movie
- Learning to value privacy over loneliness
- Learning to like your own company

Sorting all this out with honesty takes some serious interior conversation. This process is cleverly reflected in one woman's (she preferred to remain anonymous) essay about the familiar solo problem of sleeping alone.

Sleeping Single in a Double Bed

Suddenly single. Death, divorce, separations of all kinds just happen. Life's natural subtractions leave many of us as *one*—whole, maybe, but often feeling splintered.

And there's no shortage of advice about this condition—how to cook for one, how to keep loneliness at bay, how to negotiate for health insurance, how to meet new people. But somehow no one ever mentions what it's like to wake up at 3 a.m. with the old country-western lament ringing in your ears: "I'm sleeping single in a double bed."

They say that alone is not the same as lonely. Granted, that's true, but sometimes in the middle of a big wide bed in the middle of a frosty night, they feel the same. And the unvarnished truth is that I miss the bristle of an unshaven face, the otherness of a male body, the joy of putting my icy feet against someone's warm calves. These days I plug in the heating pad.

Like most things, though, there's another side to the story. I'll admit to some major compensations to this sleeping alone business. During one of those inevitable sleepless nights of flipping and flopping, it's a relief to have the whole mattress to contain my restlessness. There are no snores to break the silence; no one pulls the covers off or invades my territory or crowds me to the edge of the mattress. And I can pile on as many blankets as I want … or as few.

Nowadays, I often have some underage companions. It's a singular experience to sense the delicious presence of a sweet-smelling, cuddly grandchild gently touching my face at 6 a.m., whispering, "Is it time to get up yet, Nanna?" Tender moments, indeed.

But even with the exhilarating freedom of having all that room to myself, some nights I yearn for the magical other, the coziness of two bodies nestled like spoons. Yes, there are moments when it's difficult to sleep alone in a king-size bed, especially without a king.

Setting Boundaries

Running a close second to loneliness in the category of challenges was the problem of setting boundaries. "I can't do what I used to be able to do, and it's hard to make my peace with that," explained Henry. Whether they were unable to climb a ladder, dance a jig, or manage three grandchildren at once, people in later life regretted the loss of energy, stamina, manual dexterity, and mobility. Addressing such realities pointed to a difficult set of decisions: that of setting boundaries.

"I knew I had to make some changes," said Denise, "but I didn't want to disappoint anyone. Or maybe the problem was that I didn't want to disappoint myself. Either way, as I've gotten older, I require more rest and more peace and quiet than in younger years. Finally, it dawned on me that I wouldn't be any use to anyone if I didn't take better care of myself, and that meant learning how to say no."

Seventy-year-old Clara's parents were in their nineties, and she was exhausted by caretaking demands. "I want to be there for them at this time in their lives, but this year both my husband and

I are experiencing physical challenges of our own. There isn't enough of me to go around, it seems, and not enough energy to get it all done. I rarely get to see my grandchildren, I'm too tired to go to choir practice, my house and yard are in a mess, and my fatigue is becoming chronic. But, there I go—blaming the situation and complaining about it instead of taking responsibility for what I can do about it."

Near emotional and physical burnout, she made some tough choices.

- She got her parents settled in an assisted living facility nearby and limited her visits (when possible) to once a week.
- She took a leave of absence from the choir.
- She and her husband began to explore the possibilities for downsizing and simplifying their own living arrangements.
- She hired whatever temporary help for yard and house chores they could afford.
- Drawer by drawer, closet by closet, they began the process of sorting and sharing their belongings.
- She developed a plan to eat healthier, get adequate rest, and take a short daily walk to keep the oxygen flowing.

Setting boundaries involved some risks and rewards. "I was afraid my family wouldn't consider me useful anymore, as if I were more a burden than a help. I wanted to live up to their expectations and meet their needs, like I always had," reported Pauline. "What I discovered, though, was that I was actually trying to fulfill my own expectations of myself or what I mistakenly thought God required of me. I thought I wasn't worth much unless I performed like a superwoman. I had to risk their disappointment, but they didn't react that way at all! When I finally let go of all those perceived expectations, I was able to state the truth honestly without whining. What a relief."

Setting boundaries also carried some surprising rewards. John made this interesting observation: "In a strange way, telling the truth gave me an unexpected bonus. Somehow, declaring my own limits enabled my children to trust my judgment. They saw that even though I'm more physically limited than I used to be, I'm still capable of seeing the situation clearly and making wise choices for myself. I think my continued denial or attempt to exceed my capabilities would make them wonder if I was still in charge of my faculties! In an unspoken way, not ignoring my own limits provided surprising security to my family. I didn't expect that."

Stephen had been founder and facilitator of a successful family business, retiring willingly in his late seventies. He was precise about the boundaries he preferred during his retirement years as he told his sons and daughters, "The business is now yours, but I still want to be involved. What I would like is to come in to work a half day on Tuesdays and Thursdays and be a kind of advisor— a 'wise old man.' How do you feel about that?" His straightforward attitude paved the way for relevant discussions about how to structure the new company management and division of responsibilities.

"Holidays have always been held at my house—sort of like the Currier and Ives Christmas cards," laughed Lucille. "I loved to host the family gatherings—not just Thanksgiving and Christmas, but birthdays, betrothals, graduations—you name it, I made it happen. Over the years, other family members started helping with the food, but now even preparing the tables and getting the house in welcoming order began to wear me out."

A gifted and enthusiastic cook, Lucille was almost eighty when she set some boundaries. It was clearly time to pass the torch to the younger folks. "I told my children and grandchildren I had developed a chronic condition called 'stamina shortage,'" she declared with a wink. "I admitted that I was no longer invincible and couldn't host the future feasts, but I could always produce a couple of my family-famous pecan pies. It felt good to tell the truth about my own energy level."

Perhaps the deepest reward for setting boundaries is that it allows us to move from "they need me to" to "this is what I'm able to do," from "I ought to" to "I choose to," and from "I have to" to "I want to." Healthy honoring of our own needs doesn't imply a selfish or noncaring attitude. Rather, it patterns for others a realistic connection to yourself and models honest family relationships—with no pretending, no guilt, no shoulds, no oughts.

Where you are is where you are; where you are going is up to you.

Tying Your Shoes and Giving Up the Car

"Bending over to tie my shoes is a double whammy for me," laughed Roger. "Surgery on my back last year left me with a limited range of motion, and the arthritis in my fingers limited my dexterity. Doesn't sound like a big deal, right? Well, believe me, it *can* be. I used to start every day in a grumpy mood, and I got tired of hearing myself complain. So I decided to devise a system for dealing with this kind of stuff."

"What do you mean—a system?" I asked.

"Well, first, I tell myself: it is as it is, and that's that. Then I think about ways that I can make it better. For instance, to deal with my shoe-tying problem, I got one of those dandy long-handled shoehorns so I wouldn't have to bend over so far. Then I threw my lace-up shoes in the closet and bought some sneakers with simple Velcro tab closings and a nice pair of loafers. Made all the difference in the world.... I'm so thankful someone was clever enough to invent these things. I discovered a whole host of gizmos that have made my life easier, like a soft-grip jar opener. Just yesterday I bought a fancy, battery-operated gadget that uncorks my wine bottles!"

Clara told a similar story. "I've been a pretty fast mover all my life," she told me, "always tearing around in a hurry to get to the next thing. Well, last year I got a little ahead of myself and ended up with a broken hip. Boy, did that ever slow me down! I left rehab with a walker and a cranky attitude. I was a pain in the neck for quite a while till I couldn't stand myself any longer and decided to do something different. I upgraded to a fancy new walker with smooth-rolling wheels, and now I zip around almost like I used to. I even tied a big bow on it so folks could see me coming!"

Acknowledging the minuses and balancing the situation with some pluses helped many seniors maintain a sense of control when difficulties arose—even the monumental challenge of relinquishing the driver's wheel. Giving up driving seemed to be the stand-in for many unsettling losses of independence. Quite a number of folks singled it out as an issue that rocked their world.

"When I had to hand over those keys," remembered eighty-eight-year-old Clyde, "I felt as if I were handing over my life. I knew I had a long list of medical problems—failing eyesight and hearing, arthritis and the like, plenty of things that made me a menace on the road—but I couldn't admit that I was a real danger to the driving public. I'd been behind the wheel since I was fourteen, for goodness' sake, and I was a great driver!"

For Clyde, giving up the car was tantamount to giving in to dying. Even when he began to notice the frequency of near misses and close calls, he refused to cooperate with his concerned family. Finally, a minor fender bender (which could have been a major disaster) sounded the alarm bell in his head. He took a deep breath, shed a few tears, and handed over the keys.

One of the most creative schemes for dealing with this transition involved a family who decided to give this loss the acknowledgment and attention it deserved. Rory had been a car lover all his life—collecting and restoring old cars, going to automobile races, and reveling in long road trips. His children and grandchildren hosted a party to honor Rory's relationship with his cars and ease the transition for him.

Friends and family gathered all the old photos they could find of Rory and his cars and put them in a special scrapbook, listing each car and the years in which he drove it. They told hilarious stories of road trips and memorable vacations with an emphasis on the car that provided their transportation. One person made a poster listing the advantages of being carless: no automobile insurance premiums, no costly repairs, no frosty windshields to scrape. Then each person provided a clever IOU coupon to celebrate the change: three taxi rides, ten visits to the doctor, a trip to the grocery store each Tuesday, valet service to the restaurant of his choice. They even topped off the evening with a giant cake in the shape of a car.

It also helps if the transition to "carlessness" can be done gradually. "First I stopped driving at night," said Earl. "Then, no more out-of-town trips. Then, only right turns to nearby locations. Then, allowing others to drive while I occupied the passenger seat. Easing into it over several months seemed to make it a little less formidable."

One surprising observation surfaced more than once. Many who had already experienced the loss of the car commented on the importance of family members not downplaying the event. "When they act as if it's a ho-hum occurrence, it hurts," commented Edith. "Saying, 'Oh, you'll be fine, it's nothing,' just makes you feel worse. Those around you need to affirm your feelings of loss—because no longer being in control of your transportation is lots bigger than getting out of the driver's seat. It's about much more than the car itself."

Acknowledging the changes—whether they're daily irritants or once-in-a-lifetime bombshells—can open the way for making peace with them.

Sleeping Dilemmas

"Our first words to each other in the morning are almost always 'Did you sleep well?'" said Sandra and Clarence. "When did getting a good night's sleep become such a challenge?"

This sentiment was echoed by dozens of respondents. Changes in sleep patterns, snoring, obsessing about problems at 3 a.m., frequent bathroom visits—all pointed to a problem that plagues many of us in later life. "We love each other very much," added Sandra, "but we finally admitted that occasionally we enjoy sleeping in separate beds so we can get a better night's rest. It was a relief to know that we both felt the same way!"

At lunch with a group of women friends, Anna related a conversation that developed when one person confessed that she preferred sleeping alone at this stage in her life. The chorus of me-toos evoked some hearty laughter and a realization that their condition was probably universal. Women voiced this opinion much more often than men did, usually accompanied by familiar complaints about snoring husbands.

Kathy (not her real name), a writer, expressed her frustrations in a clever and insightful poem, which she gave me permission to quote. It pretty much says it all:

SEPARATE BEDS
The marriage bed,
where two became one,
where pillow talk soothed away secret cares,
where earlier heated words were cooled and put to rest,
where after separate daytime lives,
the two returned to one resting place.

But now,
sleep apnea,
restless limbs,
urgent bodily needs
arrive unbidden.
Unwelcome guests
sharing the bed meant for two.

A quiet tiptoe to the spare room,
only this once, he says.
Ah, the relief of good sleep,
she murmurs,
as twice becomes thrice and more.

Jolted and bereft, he laments,
Is this what it's come to?
even as he guiltily savors the spaciousness to stretch.

Time to let go of an ideal vision
that never allows change, she says.
Time to let reality in,
time to savor the gift of sleep
and meet again in the morning,
to stumble sleepily into the cuddle-spoon embrace that awaits.
Two returning to the one marriage bed,
now refreshed and renewed.

Fear and Faith

> *There is no fear in love, but perfect love casts out fear.*
> 1 JOHN 4:18

"What if I fall in the middle of the night? Who will find me? What will I do?" Sue was voicing the fear of many of us in our advancing years, especially those who live alone. As illness and death take on a startling reality, fear moves from a vague concept to a frightening particularity. What was once felt as an underlying anxiety takes on precise characteristics. Here are some of the specific concerns mentioned by those I interviewed:

- Traveling alone, with the complexity of new rules and regulations
- Getting lost or confused on solo road trips
- Vulnerability to crime
- Finding yourself far away from familiar doctors and good medical facilities
- Tripping, falling, breaking bones
- Being viewed as a helpless, dependent old fogey

"Going around scared all the time is no way to live," stated Richard. "I found myself staying at home more and more, rather than taking the chance of being vulnerable. My TV and computer became my links to the world, and I didn't want to become a hermit. I had to take the bull by the horns and make some changes."

Richard got a security alarm installed and made himself wear a heart monitor suited to his precarious heart condition. After several months, he decided to move to an assisted living facility where he could have more interaction with others.

One of the fears underneath the fears turned out to be the reluctance to ask for help, the assumption that you were imposing on others. Matilda expressed that underlying anxiety by saying shyly, "I just didn't want to be trouble to my friends and family. Then one friend really set me straight by saying, 'Well, if you never ask *me* for help, I won't feel free to ask *you* when I need it!' That conversation led to some pretty dramatic changes for our whole group of single women."

She described their intricate arrangement. They called it their "Emergency Calling Circle," a proactive response to their fears of being alone in a personal emergency. Most of their relatives lived in other cities and were not readily available, so they made a serious covenant with one another to be "first responders," remaining until a family member could arrive and take over. One of the computer-savvy women collected the necessary details and e-mailed the information to the six women in the group. Each willingly provided the following:

- Primary physician, with phone numbers
- Preferred hospital (compatible with the insurance)
- All insurance numbers and information
- Blood type and allergies
- List of current medications and dosages
- Family members to be notified, complete with contact information

"Taking positive action did a lot to mitigate our fear," added Matilda. "We didn't sit around wringing our hands being pitiful little old ladies. We did something about it."

In most cases, dealing effectively with fear took time, focus, and intention. Fear usually wants to act too soon, to frantically seek a solution to the anxiety—medication, changing locations, remarrying just for the sake of companionship, moving in with the children. Worthwhile solutions were most often found within the bonds of community and in reconnecting with faith.

Clara and Ruth were frequent movie companions, determined not to become housebound. Each lived in an apartment in the midtown section of their city where crime of all sorts was a frequent occurrence. They made a habit of calling each other to check in after they had been out for the evening. And these spunky seniors even enrolled in a self-defense class.

These stories illustrate the significant difference between needless worry and appropriate concern. Worry about growing older is fruitless; we can't do a thing to change the fact of it. Fretting over things that can't be changed amounts to swimming constantly in a pool of anxiety that depletes body and spirit.

When a concern is legitimate, however, taking appropriate action not only helps alleviate the situation, but it's also personally empowering. The feeling of helplessness experienced by many in later life melts away when positive action is taken. They begin to recognize the value of interdependency.

James offered this perspective: "You know, most of us were brought up to stand on our own two feet. Independence was a cardinal virtue in my family, so to ask for help makes me feel vulnerable and desperate. Even though it goes against the grain, it's pretty stupid not to ask for help when you need it."

But what about the free-floating fears that accompany radical changes in later life—sudden illness, loss of a spouse, unexpected financial distress, mental decline—those times when life as we know it shakes and cracks under our feet? Faith provides that solid ground that exists under the cracks, a foundation under the rubble. Flora Wuellner—pastor, writer, and mentor to many (including me)—wrote eloquently of her own response to these self-shattering times:

> When I am faced with challenge and feel gripped by anxiety ... when my heart speeds up, when my breathing is tight as I open that letter, wait for that phone call, sit in the doctor's office waiting for those test results, scan the bank statement, face a difficult personal encounter, experience a loss, admit a serious mistake, I try inwardly to stand up, raise my head, and look straight at the possibility of a changed personal world. Then I remind myself that at that very moment when the ground trembles and my old securities pass away, God is with me.... Where will that hand take me this time? What new life is opening up?[2]

One of aging's most profound fears, however, seems beyond the realm of hopeful thinking—and that is the possibility of dementia and its related maladies. We try to make light of it with clever jokes about misplacing the car keys or quips such as "Of all the things I've lost, I miss my mind the most," but we know it's no laughing matter. Our humor never quite masks the fear it tries to hide. Dealing with Alzheimer's and other mind-related conditions involves yet another layer of the aging experience and is one of the most difficult obstacles to a peaceful later life. Whether we are patients or caretakers, the challenges are overwhelming and terrifying. Because the subject is beyond both the scope of this book and the breadth of my experience, I've included a number of sources in the suggestions for further reading that may be of help to those who draw this unlucky card.

When all is said and done, I know this much: fear is a part of the human condition; it goes with the territory. As such, it is both natural and problematic. It can motivate but also paralyze. It can protect us but also make us overly cautious. Ultimately, when we are willing to face and acknowledge the fear, it can serve as a doorway toward the healing power on the other side.

Faith that God can take any disaster that comes to us and help us pick up the pieces produces the peace that passes all understanding, which I like to define as "deep rest in a sea of unrest." This assurance can gird our lives with strength and hope, even when that sea is stormy. Moving to that level of trust involves cultivating a faith that can sustain us in the "dark night" of the aging soul. Developing personal spiritual disciplines, reading inspiring literature, being in community with kindred spirits, and being agents of grace to others can help build that trust, brick by brick, moment by moment.

Later life offers us the time to search for meaning in the midst of mayhem—and hopefully the faith to find it.

Fallacies of Forgiveness

When I asked the question about any lingering forgiveness issues, one story made me catch my breath.

"Years ago, when our nineteen-year-old daughter was murdered, my crash course in forgiveness began," remembered Walter. "It was quite an odyssey. I didn't think it was possible to do it, but it was. I had to see forgiveness as a process, not a one-time act. If I treated it as an event, it was too easy to fail, to admit defeat, to say, 'I tried, but I just couldn't do it.' It's closer to the truth to say, 'I'm willing to begin the *process* of forgiveness.'"

First, he realized, he had to acknowledge what the anger was doing to him—to his body as well as his spirit. "I remember someone telling me that 'resentment hurts the vessel in which it is stored more than the object on which it is poured,'" he said. "Anger that is kept alive year after year does its toxic work on us. It's like scratching poison ivy—at first it feels good to scratch it, but all that does is spread the poison."

Walter admitted that the process took time. "I had to feel and own the anger and rage before I could begin to let it go," he recalled. "Even then, it was impossible to do it alone under my own steam. How could God forgive such a horrible thing—or expect me to forgive it? I had to wrestle with that for quite a while. My faith in God's forgiveness had to be strengthened and reaffirmed. I prayed the Lord's Prayer, especially the part about 'Forgive us our trespasses as we forgive those who trespass against us.' I read everything I could find that mentioned forgiveness—like the words of Jesus on the cross forgiving his own murderers."

Walter envisioned God's forgiveness as a rolling river, an ongoing reality of love. "We don't have to produce it ourselves," he added, "but we have to be willing to participate in it. It felt to me as if I were taking my boat and paddle and entering a river of forgiveness that was stronger than I was. What I needed to contribute was willingness, not power."

Another realization helped Walter's progress on the path to forgiveness. "At first, it seemed that if I forgave the murderer, I was somehow condoning what he did, saying that it was okay, that it didn't hurt that badly. And that was unimaginable, of course. I had to reframe it, to understand that we forgive people, not behaviors. And forgiveness is not forgetting, either. What I was really saying was that I didn't want to carry that burden of unforgiveness inside me any longer; it was destroying me."

In addition to this dramatic and difficult story of forgiveness, I encountered many whose forgiveness issues were directed toward themselves. "I made so many mistakes as a mother, and I can't do it over," recalled Sandra. "I loved my children, but honestly, it's hard to forgive myself for my own damaging words and deeds."

Remorse was reflected by Peter also. "It's hard to excuse some of the things I've done in my life. But we human beings are good at whitewashing our actions, justifying them with all sorts of rationalizations to get ourselves off the hook. Now that I'm older, it seems healthier to admit that most all of us have done some pretty rotten things, often from ignorance, sometimes out of anger and malice, and frequently with motives of self-interest—indulging our passions or trying to make ourselves look better at someone else's expense. But when we have the courage to stare our own demons in the face and admit them, the pathway of forgiveness seems to open up."

Marsha's comments on forgiveness had to do with the necessity of releasing the outcome. "It's unilateral," she insisted. "You can't control other people's responses, if you choose to forgive them. They may or may not want to move toward reconciliation with you. The point is, you can't let the littleness in others bring out the littleness in you."

One final word of wisdom came from Hannah, who mentioned the relationship between unforgiveness and martyrdom. "If you live long enough with an unforgiving attitude, it becomes part of your identity," she said emphatically. "You become a permanent victim, wearing it like a badge of honor. I had to quit chewing on the hurt and stop talking about it. Only then could I move toward forgiveness. Otherwise, I was sabotaging myself."

Writer and theologian Frederick Buechner's graphic description of the condition of unforgiveness provides powerful motivation to move beyond it:

> Of the Seven Deadly Sins, anger is possibly the most fun. To lick your wounds, to smack your lips over grievances long past, to roll over your tongue the prospect of bitter confrontations still to come, to savor to the last toothsome morsel both the pain you are given and the pain you are giving back—in many ways it is a feast fit for a king. The chief drawback is that what you are wolfing down is yourself. The skeleton at the feast is you.[3]

Accepting the Life You've Lived

As a former golfer, I appreciate the words of Benedictine nun Joan Chittister in her *Gift of Years*: "Regret is ... the sand trap of the soul."[4]

And it seems that many of us are caught in that sand trap in our later years. Letting go of our dreams for our lives is quite a feat when many of those dreams didn't come true. One of the major challenges of aging is to accept who we are and where we have been, rather than mourn the life that was ours. Our dreams for ourselves sit in our unconscious minds like resident fixtures, underneath the articulated agendas. Unfortunately, we usually measure our happiness by their fulfillment—or lack of it.

"My life hasn't panned out like I planned," mused Carolyn. "I thought it would be carefree and uncluttered by the time I reached middle age. Instead, my grown daughter is still living at home, my son and grandchildren are traumatized by divorce, and my aging parents need constant monitoring. Unless I can find meaning in the downs as well as the ups, these last years of life will feel like a gigantic letdown."

Carolyn and her husband decided, in their words, to "put on another pair of glasses." Determined not to get stuck in regrets, they shifted their focus. "The truth is, we've learned to treasure a quiet evening at home together more than a trip on the Orient Express," exclaimed Dave. "There's more joy in appreciating what is than in complaining about what might have been."

Others were having similar struggles:

- "My wife and I thought we would grow old together, surrounded by a bevy of grandchildren, but our son and daughter live in California now. They're both married and have great careers but don't plan to have kids of their own."
- "I never intended for the last half of my life to be controlled by diabetes!"
- "All I ever wanted was to have a good, solid marriage. After two divorces and the advancing years, I know it isn't going to happen."
- "Why didn't I go back to college when I had the chance? Now I'll never be the English professor I wanted to be."
- "I dreamed of standing on that ridge and looking down on Machu Picchu in Peru and now it's too late. My heart condition couldn't cope with the altitude."

Teri had her own set of regrets, but got sick of the sadness. Her proactive solution made good sense. "I guess it's okay to name the regrets and feel the disappointment, but I didn't want to *live there*," she remarked. "My life was passing me by while I was busy complaining. I finally wrote down every good thing that I could remember—the sweet moments, the relationships that *did* work, the growth that came with the struggles. Then I started monitoring my own thoughts and words. Every time I heard myself whining, I got out that list and shifted my focus to the good stuff."

Though I felt I had confronted the issues of letting go during midlife (I even wrote a book about it), one area was hidden from me. It took years to realize that I was clutching my dream for my life in a tight fist inside me. So powerful was my determination to be a "successful" wife and mother that I might set the dream on a shelf temporarily, but I never really let it go. In my mind at that time, that role was the feminine ideal and anything else was second best. I described the struggle from that perspective to real freedom like this:

> In my head, I knew I was complete without being the perfect wife and mother. After all, I reasoned, I was not called by God to be perfect; I was called to be faithful and to live in utter openness of spirit. But I wanted my heart to accept this, to soften its stubborn stance. So things hadn't worked out the way I'd planned. So what? I was tired of being weighed down with expectations. I wanted to be *free*....
>
> But to do that ... I had to change my life questions: 'What next? How can my mistakes be used? How can I make my life count in new ways?' As I took the first tentative steps into those threatening questions, I slowly began to live into the answers, one minute at a time. It was as if I ceased trying to do it all by myself. I allowed God to help me pick up the shattered pieces of my life and begin to construct a new mosaic—one with new colors

and unexpected patterns.... I was ready to walk into the years left to me with open hands, not with a death grip on my own agenda for happiness, clutching my limited definition of who I was and who I could become.[5]

Occasionally, people stumbled on the matter of fairness, of getting what you "deserved." Statements such as "She didn't deserve that many hard knocks in her life," or "He was such a rascal, yet here he is, surrounded by success," challenge our need for fairness. Writer and pastor Steve Garnaas-Holmes has an enlightening theological perspective on the matter:

At some level we believe that there is such a thing as "deserving," that somehow God or the universe keeps score of our past choices and then later rewards or punishes us for them. This is not true. Neither good fortune nor bad is a sign of anything but luck. (Workers are exploited ... cheaters win ... saints get cancer ... good things happen to bad people and vice versa.) But our poor little egos, running on our logical [left] brains, can't get this, since they see everything in terms of predictability, formulas, cause and effect. So they just pretend that it's true anyway. And we live our lives chasing and being chased by guilt and [unworthiness]. We live false lives, and the person we really are perishes.

[We're invited] to jump off that not-so-merry-go-round that goes nowhere. "Repent," we are told. To repent doesn't mean to jump back on the reward-and-punishment merry-go-round only on a more righteous horse. It means to go a new way. It means to "turn," to head in a different direction, and as we do, we "turn," we change.

To repent means to turn away from the illusion of rewards and punishment.... To repent is to join God in the present moment.

Certainly, we turn from evil and selfish ways. But not in order to get a better grade. We do it because God is pure compassion, and as we turn to God we are turned into God's reflection.[6]

Those who made the difficult move from regret to acceptance learned to release the past and relish the present moment. Edith said it like this: "This may not be the life I expected, but I've made my peace with the one I got—with a healthy dose of gratitude thrown in."

Looking Inside

1. Has loneliness been a part of later life for you? In what way? What was most helpful to you during those times?

2. In what relationships are your boundaries porous? What price do you pay for this?

3. How does fear manifest itself in your life? Have you been able to discuss this with anyone with an eye toward solutions?

4. Name one wonderful memory and one terrible memory that stand out in your life up to now. How might you accept them equally, as part of the whole of life?

Surprising Gifts

The gift of these years is not merely being alive—it is the gift of becoming more fully alive than ever.
JOAN CHITTISTER

People are always talking about the rigors of growing old, saying things like 'It isn't for sissies' or 'Just you wait, you can't imagine what it's like.' That may be true sometimes, but what about the glories of getting older—the joy, the freedom, the gratitude? Believe me, there's some *gold* in the golden years, if we'll just dig for it," insisted Charlotte. And a number of her late-life peers agreed.

When I asked folks what they liked best about the years past seventy, they usually broke into a smile first before saying a single word. Though their answers were wide-ranging, no one was stumped by the question. They were simply surprised to be asked. Naming the challenges was a much more frequent focus than identifying the gifts.

Being Real

"Oh, the blessed relief of finally being happy in my own skin," reflected Norene. "I can't believe it has taken my whole life to realize that I was allowing others to tell me who I am. Becoming what they needed or wanted or *saw* in me became the lens through which I saw myself. I had to get old before I knew that no one could really tell me who I am unless I allowed it."

Self-knowledge calls us to become more responsible than most of us wish to be. Many sink into the pervasive pattern of needing the approval and reassurance of others. None of us is immune to this need. Though I hoped I had conquered that particular demon as I aged, I found that the need for approval never really goes away. It is always lurking around in the psyche, sneaking up behind us in a new costume. When I published my first book at age sixty-five, the feelings of vulnerability astounded me. I felt exposed, emotionally naked, and helplessly susceptible to the opinions of others. On any given day, my sense of self was bandied about by those who liked the book and those who had disagreements with it, those who thought I was a good writer and those who thought I was a pretender. The opinions of others were inflating me or deflating me—all with my permission.

It was difficult for me to withdraw that permission, but it was essential that I try. In the inventive words of educator and philosopher Howard Thurman, "Follow the grain in your own wood." It became my task to remember and rediscover what that grain actually was—who I was as a person and as a child of God—and live out of that core, no matter what applause or criticisms came my way. It was not an easy job, because the opinions of others were far from worthless. It was necessary to slowly consider each evaluation on its own merits without allowing those opinions to define me. It was necessary to learn to respond rather than react.

One of the most enduring metaphors for this kind of authenticity is Jesus's suggestion to "consider the lilies of the field, how *they* grow" (Luke 12:27). They develop slowly—turning themselves toward the Source of Light and being who they were created to be—not roses or violets, but lilies. In later life, we have the opportunity to give ourselves consciously to that same process. I keep a vase of lilies on my desk as a visual reminder.

Bonnie responded to my interview by sending her reflections via e-mail. A lively resident of a retirement facility, she
commented on authenticity in community in a particularly
enlightening way:

> I'm seventy-five. There, I've said it. Seems like a mathemat-
> ical mistake, but I was actually born in 1935. Though I've
> lived more than the traditional three-score-and-ten, I feel
> more alive, more aware, more *myself* than ever before.
> Here's one of the things I like about this age—I'm surrounded
> by lots of high-functioning older adults, and that really
> helps. Sure, we occasionally forget a grandchild's name or
> where we put the keys, but there's a depth to our discus-
> sions (about *anything*) that is far more precious than conver-
> sations in our younger years. We don't waste valuable time
> on small talk anymore. And there's an added serendipity:
> the more I have the courage to be myself, the more I allow
> others to be themselves. We don't have to compete or
> deserve each other's friendship; we don't have to convince
> or persuade or win the argument. We figure we've earned
> the right to be wrong, so we tell as many failure stories as
> success stories. They're more interesting, anyway. We cut
> each other lots of slack, especially when we agree to dis-
> agree and end it with a hug. Don't let people tell you that
> growing old is all bad; it has many hidden bonuses.

There were noticeable gender differences along the road to being
real. Many men were relieved to be free of society's measure of
success after a lifetime of being focused on vocation. Women
generally felt liberated from the need to constantly adapt to the
requests and requirements of others—though many had to move
beyond the deeply ingrained belief that self-care is selfish. Being
real and being kind need not be mutually exclusive.

"Being true to myself is not saying, 'I'll do what I want to do
and to heck with everyone else,'" insisted Gloria. "I always try to

be a thoughtful person, but my motivation is different now. I'm no longer kind so I can win others' approval or look like a good person. I want to do the loving thing, because that's who God has shown me to be in my best, deepest self. If I'm going to live out of that essence, I have to take care of myself physically and spiritually, and that means telling the truth about my wants and needs and limitations."

Being real also includes letting go of the assumptions of others about who you really are. As a blonde woman from the Bible Belt—make that the buckle of the Bible Belt—I have sometimes encountered unspoken pigeonholing shaped by a Southern accent and lots of dumb-blonde jokes. In younger days, I could feel myself hoping folks would realize I had a brain. Like other women seventy and beyond, I don't care as much what people think of me. It's a liberating feature of the later years.

The Healing Power of Play

The secret of my vigor and activity is that I have managed to have a lot of fun.
LOWELL THOMAS

The participants at the Women's Retreat told me they were opening the weekend with a "Pity Party." Then I was to lead the remainder of the annual gathering on the topic of "finding the gold in the golden years." My knee-jerk reaction (as a positive Pollyanna) was utter puzzlement about their negative opening salvo. I wondered how that would fit in with the hopeful spin of my prepared material. I soon found that their lighthearted reasoning made sense.

"There are lots of things to complain about in getting older," they explained, "so we decided to get that out on the table, first thing. Instead of shoving our grievances down a rabbit hole, we're going to whine and grumble and have a big laugh over it on Friday night. Then when you start the sessions on Saturday morning, we'll be ready!"

They were right, of course. By openly carping about weight gain, memory loss, gray hair, wrinkles, and creaky joints (to name a few), they cleared the way for another point of view. Exposing their complaints to the light of friendship and humor took most of the steam out of the angst. They laughed themselves silly with negative one-upmanship and had a rollicking time. Of course, it wasn't long before the commiseration dissolved into companionship and the communal hilarity became a healing fountain.

As human beings, it feels good to scratch an itch—whether it's poison ivy or an internal toxin—especially in the company of folks who understand what you're talking about. That's why all those terrible greeting cards about the horrors of old age sell like hotcakes. The load is lightened for everyone, because the burden is shared with good-natured humor. In the words of British writer G. K. Chesterton, "Angels can fly because they take themselves so lightly."

Laura offered a personal version of the Pity Party. "When I'm upset about something, I get my kitchen timer," she said with a twinkle in her eye. "I give myself twenty minutes to grouse about it, and when that timer rings, I'm done. I don't want that poison in my system."

A friend of mine with an irrepressible joie de vivre found a way to infuse even the trials of breast cancer with her own brand of humor. "When I entered the hospital for the mastectomy, I made my little personal nest, complete with makeup and earrings," reported Pat. "Then as soon as I could focus my eyes after the surgery, I put my pearls on."

Out of her own healing experiences with humor came an ongoing project known as "Pat's Pearls," a pouch she created that contains a string of pearls and a card. She gives the pouch to the hospital's cancer patients, who borrow her witty symbol of recovery, then return the pearls to the hospital when they are discharged. That kind of playful perspective is delightfully contagious.

Many seniors spoke of the need to reconsider their definition of fun at this stage in their lives. Ellen and Edgar reported that gallivanting around the globe didn't hold as much delight for them now as gathering their extended family for an evening of hamburgers on the grill. Marsha mentioned her new habit of taking her grandchildren on a "treasure walk." Each child is given a basket for containing unusual rocks, colorful leaves, and wildflowers. "While we're strolling slowly, I enjoy listening to their offhand chatter much more than the stilted, polite answers they normally give me when I'm firing questions at them."

Striking a balance between playing too hard and hardly playing can be a challenging task for those in later life. "Act your age" can be appropriate when you're thirty-five, but it may be a mistake at seventy, when it is often used as an excuse for laziness. Yet, some things are truly beyond our budgets or our bodies, and thoughtful decisions are in order.

Several years ago, honesty demanded that I admit I was past going to midnight New Year's Eve parties. On the other hand, I wasn't past celebrating the beginning of a brand-new year. I merely had to find a different way to mark the occasion. An early, informal gathering suited me best, so I sent the following invitation to friends:

> At six, it is New Year's in London,
> At seven, they dance in Paree;
> At eight, "Auld Lang Syne" spans the ocean,
> As the QE-2 hosts a party at sea!
> So drop by in a tux or a T-shirt;
> In jeans or jewels, as you please.
> Each hour as the bell marks midnight somewhere,
> You can toast the New Year at your ease.

Those who were headed to a late celebration continued to other venues, and the early birds among us observed the holiday at our preferred hour. And everyone was out of my house by 9 o'clock.

Roy was determined to push through his knee pain with gritted teeth to maintain his spot in a weekly tennis foursome. When the price of pain became too high, however, he had the good sense to shift gears. He joined a walking and biking group to maintain some athletic camaraderie, and his relieved knees said thank you.

There's no doubt that laughter feeds our fun and fuels our bodies, even when the hilarity is at our own expense. Mary offered this comical take on the problem of spinach between her teeth:

> I'm not sure when my mouth began to rearrange its furniture. Wrinkles and bulges I expected, but gaps around my gums? Who could have known? These tiny crevices seem to snag just about anything that wanders by, but they must have special magnets for spinach. Dark green tidbits love to lodge there, turning a satisfying smile into a dreadful distraction. I'm convinced that sending a silent signal to a friend that she has spinach in her teeth is a litmus test of love.

So remember to laugh a little. In the famous words of Irish playwright George Bernard Shaw, "We don't stop playing because we grow old; we grow old because we stop playing."

Gratitude Is More Than a Thank-You Note

If the only prayer you ever say in life is "thank you," this is enough.
MEISTER ECKHART

I thought I knew what gratitude was until I started trying to write a book about it. Saying thank you in one way or another is a common thread among all sentient beings, not to mention animals. Not only do babies giggle their thanks, but dogs wag their tails and cats purr. What could be more natural? The first phrases you learn in any foreign language class are *muchas gracias, merci beaucoup, danke schoen.* The impulse seems built into the created order, and we human beings are wired for it. Yet, it's difficult to define gratitude adequately.

Proper upbringing in our culture usually includes the habits of offering grace at meals, saying thank you often and on cue, and being able to write a decent thank-you note. Yet, all of these behaviors echo the customary context of gratitude: the affirmation of what is going well in our lives—the things that bring us pleasure, the things we consider blessings.

Those I spoke with were well acquainted with a broader horizon of thanksgiving, because later life propels us there. In the words of Cheryl, "Do you cease to be a grateful person when everything goes wrong? When tragedy strikes? When prayers seem unanswered? When Lady Luck is nowhere to be found? An attitude of gratitude can't be dependent on easy sailing. It has to be more than that."

The importance of thankfulness is affirmed, not only in all sacred texts, but by contemporary science as well. Studies are showing conclusively that gratitude is good for us: grateful people live more fruitful and happy lives; thanksgiving unleashes positive hormones into our bodies; immune systems are boosted by optimistic emotions; relationships blossom when nurtured by appreciation. You name it—gratitude helps it.

Raymond called this positive tendency his "gratitude muscle." He offered several ways to keep that muscle toned. "If my gratitude muscle gets flabby, I get cranky and sour and depressed. I try to build that muscle, one thought at a time, one word at a time, one action at a time. It's kind of fun. This may seem silly, but I even keep a small rock in my pocket called my gratitude rock; every time I reach in my pocket, it reminds me to be grateful for something."

Fay started watching her own words. "When I noticed all my language of complaint, I was appalled," she recounted. "My friends and I know the statistics about the importance of being thankful, and we've read the Bible verses, yet we frequently play 'Ain't it awful?' It's like an insidious downward spiral—from a simple comment about the lousy traffic to out-of-control debt to ill-mannered children to creaky joints and on to the sorry state of the world.

What I began to notice was that I was far from an innocent observer in this whining process. I willingly joined in the chorus of complaint with my own set of gripes."

We don't have to join the insidious game of "ain't it awful." Rita made a conscious decision not to play. "I decided to refrain from joining the grumbling voices around me, to remain silent when something or someone was being trashed by others. I didn't need to preach or judge or chastise the complainers. I could simply offer a word of gratitude and hope, or merely avoid joining the negative fray."

Lou came to a similar realization. "When I decided to widen the lens of my gratitude, I knew I had to find a way to include all of life, not just the good stuff," he said. "I realized how much I had learned through the things that didn't work—the failures, the stumblings, the twists and turns. I guess now I'm just thankful to be alive, to realize that God is with me in all my ups and downs and will be my firm foundation, no matter what. Here's an image that speaks to me. I think about grace like a big beach ball that's half black and half white bobbing up and down in the water. It's floating securely in something larger, buoyant, sustaining, empowering, uplifting. That circular ball of grace contains both the light and the dark moments and may get tossed around, but it doesn't sink."

True thanksgiving isn't just being aware of your blessings or affirming what is working in your life. That's certainly valid, but what can we do about those times when things are *not* working? Author and theologian Henri Nouwen put beautiful words to this dilemma:

> How often we tend to divide our past into good things to remember with gratitude and painful things to accept or forget.... We develop a mentality in which we hope to collect more good memories than bad.... Gratitude in its deepest sense means to live life as a gift to be received gratefully. But gratitude as the gospel speaks about it embraces all of life: the good and the bad, the joyful and the painful, the holy and the not so holy....

It is so easy for me to put the bad memories under the rug of my life and to think only about the good things that please me. By doing so, however, I prevent myself from discovering the joy beneath my sorrow, the peace hidden in the midst of my conflicts, and the strength that becomes visible in the midst of my weakness.... As long as we remain resentful about things that we wish had not happened, about relationships that we wish had turned out differently, about mistakes we wish we had not made, part of our heart remains isolated, unable to bear fruit in the new life ahead of us.[1]

Eric spoke of how his feeling about gratitude had evolved through the years. "I used to think 'being thankful in all things' was just a glorified game of 'let's pretend,'" he remembered. "Then I made the distinction between being thankful *in* all things rather than *for* all things. It was possible to feel the pain of whatever was going on, to affirm that 'it is as it is,' then grab a grateful thought—maybe a tiny silver thread of hope—and affirm that also, even if it's saying, 'I'm grateful I made it through this dismal day.' Somehow that shift opened me up to a perspective of thanksgiving underneath all the troubling events."

Strengthening our "gratitude muscle" is a conscious choice. We can allow the challenges of life to break us down or break us open. When thanksgiving becomes a natural part of who we are, we quit judging so much, our complaining lessens, our worries decrease, people enjoy our company, and we can be used by God more fruitfully. We can literally become walking, talking gratitude, as it becomes more who we are than what we do— just like the bundle of joy visited in the hospital by Rev. John Claypool:

I remember ... calling on two parishioners in their middle eighties, and each was up against an enormous array of physical difficulties. When I entered the first lady's room, I immediately sensed that she was badly depressed by her situation and she lost little time in cataloguing her complaints to me. She told me how she loathed having to leave the familiarity of her home and come to a hospital, and how it was impossible to get any sleep there because of all the interruptions day and night. She reported that the sheets on the bed were just like sandpaper, and perhaps the worst thing of all was the terrible food ... everything was true. I did my best to remind her of God's presence with her ..., but as I left, the atmosphere was still heavy ..., and I found myself drained by the whole encounter. Two floors down, I entered the room of another woman, herself aged and up against it, but I could tell from the moment I opened the door that there was a different atmosphere in that place. When I told her how sorry I was that she had to come to the hospital, she said, "Well, I'm sorry too that I have this problem, but you know, there are things that the people here can do for me that my family at home could not do. I'm grateful that places like this exist." I asked: "Do you find the commotion of the hospital disturbing to your rest?" She said, "You know, the truth is, my family at home is wonderful to me, but they have their work to do, which means I often get quite lonely.... [Here in the hospital] every time the door opens, I find myself wondering what fresh young thing is coming in now."

"Do you find the bed difficult to sleep on?" I asked.... With that her eyes brightened.... "We only change our sheets at home once a week. They change them here every day! I call that real luxury, don't you?" I remember making one last effort at consolation. "Do you find the food here hard to eat?" Again, she said, "You know, my daughter-in-law is a wonderful cook, but she tends to fix things the same way all the time, and it gets a little boring. I really enjoy the variety of the menu here." And then she added: "Eating for me under any circumstances is not easy, because I only have two teeth left. But I thank the Lord, they hit!" When she made that last statement, I felt like stepping back and giving her a full military salute. All the heroism in the world is not confined to the battlefield … the difference in the energy level in those two hospital rooms was absolutely amazing.[2]

The seniors I interviewed taught me that gratitude is not only a list of blessings but a way of being in the world, of seeing all of life through the lens of hope. Larry summed it up this way: "Here's the deal. Whatever situation you're dealing with, this is the question you ask yourself: *How am I going to see it?* The choice you make has everything to do with how things will go on from there."

Delight in the Details

> To see a world in a grain of sand and a heaven in a wild-flower, hold infinity in the palm of your hand and eternity in an hour.
>
> WILLIAM BLAKE

"One of the biggest surprises for me in this stage of life is that it's more fulfilling than I expected. I think I notice little things more," mused eighty-five-year-old Henry. "I moved pretty fast during my professional life, and I forgot to stop and smell the roses, as they say. Mind you, I loved my career, but this is different … better in a lot of ways."

One of the paradoxical gifts of later life is that, though your perspective of the world may expand, your perspective can also shrink to the universe of a spider spinning a web. A person can appreciate the vastness of the universe, yet be awestruck at the simplicity of a brilliant red cardinal against a background of snow.

In my interviews, comments like Henry's were common:

- Reading *Goodnight, Moon* to my granddaughter seems more full of life now than making a bonanza report to my CEO.
- When I am greeted by my shaggy old dog with those loving eyes and wagging tail, it just makes my day.
- The doctor said I needed to eat more slowly, and now that it isn't "gulp and run" I'm savoring the flavors.
- I never realized before that hummingbirds are so competitive until I watched them jockeying for position on the feeder.
- I'm a better listener than in my younger days; somehow, I no longer feel compelled to give a solution.

Barbara Brown Taylor described her experience of this perspective in her book *An Altar in the World*:

> Once, when I was confined to bed for the better part of a week, I spent hours watching the sunlight that came through the slats of my wooden blinds move down the white wall of my bedroom. First thing in the morning it made honey-colored rectangles with soft edges. By 10:00 a.m. the wall was striped with bands of light as straight as rulers. By noon they looked more like the rungs of a ladder, dappled with leaves from the winged elm outside my window. By 2:00 they had lost most of their character, as the sun moved over the roof of the house and left the front yard in deepening shadow.... This may sound boring to you, but it was not. It was beautiful. It was reassuring. It gave me a place outside myself to go.[3]

Sometimes the attention to detail is internal, rather than external. Claire began to notice her growing focus on the moment at hand. "I've started thinking in smaller segments, such as wondering if I can simply do the next loving thing, even if it's only letting go of all distractions when I'm listening to a friend and being present with my whole self. Dwelling in the moment seems to provide a 'vaccination' against my chronic hurry-sickness. The details blur if I rush past them."

Certain spiritual practices help this process along. "If I'm going to delight in the details," said Charles, "I must feed that part of me that experiences those feelings, like seeing with the eyes of my heart. Every night I try to fall asleep with good thoughts, replaying the day to remember four or five instances of simple joy."

As a walker, Chloe often takes what she calls a "parable walk." "It isn't a power walk; instead, I stroll very slowly," she informed me. "Then if my eye catches something, I stop and stay with it for a few minutes, really looking at it, until it teaches me. Maybe it might be a leaf letting go of its branch and floating to the ground. What do I need to let go? Or a fresh green shoot coming unexpectedly out of an old tree trunk. What in me is struggling to grow, against all odds? What divine life force is empowering it and giving me the resilience I need? Nature is a great instructor in the basics of life."

I came across an old journal entry that reflected a slow, reflective moment in my own life when the details directed me toward a deep truth.

It's my first dawn at the ocean's edge in three years. I'm a bit bleary-eyed, maybe, but alert as a sentry. I've been waiting patiently for first light for over an hour, relishing memories of sea sunrises past, turning them over in my hand like a clamshell, dwelling on the curves and contours, the beauty and the barnacles.

Oh, how this very scene, this very mixture of sand and shell and salt, has marked the seasons of my life—times of delight with sunburned toddlers, times of despair over broken relationships, times of dogged determination and irrational hope. This beach knows me and it knows my story.

Out of the corner of my eye I see a long-legged runner in pink shorts jogging across the sand, and I smile with faint recognition. I used to be that carefree creature, hair flying in the wind, heart throwing challenges at life. Inside, I still am.

That was then and this is now, yet this morning spectacle appears in its relentless rhythm. I may not be able to get the clock to stand still, but *I can*. I can sit still long enough to notice the dependable sun spreading across the horizon, the pelican diving for breakfast, the waves predictably pounding the shore. And I am breathless with trust for the Unseen Hand that turns this tide—and my own.

Time: Friend or Foe?

> *I wake each morning with a desire to save the world and a*
> *desire to savor the world; this makes it hard to plan the day.*
> E. B. WHITE

In our later years ...

The good news is we have the gift of time.

The bad news is we have the gift of time.

This paradox was illustrated repeatedly as I listened to contrasting comments from the seniors I interviewed. James offered, "I was surprised at how quickly old age arrived. The time is flying, and I want to savor every moment of it. I wish I could make the clock stand still. There just isn't enough time for me to get everything in."

Richard's viewpoint, however, was quite different. "Now I have all this time on my hands, and I don't know what to do with it. I'm not interested in constantly puttering around, doing meaningless busywork just to fill empty hours. Surely if I'm living this long, there's a good reason for it."

In her poem "The Summer Day," poet Mary Oliver challenges us to consider what we'll do with our "one wild and precious life."[4]

Quite a number of folks have chosen to reconnect with a love of learning that had been put on hold while other things claimed their attention. "In my case, the quest for knowledge has increased with age rather than decreased," commented Sylvia. "When a continuing education brochure comes in the mail, I'm like a child at Christmas," she laughed. "I sign up for things that are absolutely of no practical use to me. In fact, that's the point. Maybe all I want is to hear folks talk about a subject that I know little or nothing about and pick up a new thought or two. No tests, no term papers, nothing to prove. I don't have to have an outcome—like making money or impressing others—it's simply pure joy."

My own love affair with learning began decades ago, but in these later years, I've rekindled it. In the days before cell phones replaced tire wrenches, when stranded on the highway meant *stranded*, I took my first continuing education course on basic auto mechanics. As a single woman who traveled the highway frequently, I didn't know a fan belt from a steering wheel. Enrolling in a three-night course in car maintenance was quite daunting, but I learned how to change a flat tire with the best of them. Thank goodness I was never in a situation to test that new skill, but it was empowering to know that I could if I had to. Whether it's learning a language or getting acquainted with ancient Greece, the buffet of choices is intriguing. When I asked seventy-eight-year-old Noelle why she enrolled in an introduction to quantum physics course, she shrugged her shoulders and replied, "Oh ... just because ..."

One interviewee spoke of the change in her motivation for learning. "I realized recently that I wasn't reading for the same reasons anymore," she claimed. "In past years, I've read to keep up with trends and current books, to prepare for a book club discussion, to exercise my brain so it wouldn't atrophy—you know, the usual reasons—or to improve my pedigree. Now I just read because I *enjoy* it—because I get hooked on a good yarn or interested in how a certain author puts words together—for pure recreation. I don't feel as if I have to provide a reason. My time, my choice."

And then there are those who use this gift of time to reconnect with neglected relationships. "I've started having people over for dinner again—a pleasurable part of my life that had fallen by the wayside," testified Marie. "But now it's different. I don't need to impress my friends with gourmet cooking or a fresh-flower centerpiece. Sparkling conversation is more important to all of us than sparkling crystal. I've even let go of the social expectation of 'entertaining them because they've entertained you.' Now when I make out a guest list, I ask myself, 'Who would enjoy each other's company? Who has interests in common? Who are *real people* rather than social caricatures?' It has made for some very stimulating evenings, whether we get a pizza delivered or everyone brings a dish. The point is relationship rather than razzle-dazzle."

Still others focus on reconnecting with the world and finding ways to be of service to others. "My wife and I have decided that 'wise old man' and 'crone' are not pejorative terms at all," joked Carl. "We like being approached with respect for the wisdom of our years. The elderly have been valued in indigenous cultures for centuries, though not so much in America."

"Not that we waited for opportunities to knock at our door," added Mary. "We sought out venues where we could offer what we have. As a former lawyer, Carl volunteers at the local legal aid office, and I use my social services background to work with abused women. Besides, it helps us more than it helps them."

Frederick Buechner's famous formula for service has provided guidance for many searching for a way to give back to society. He identified your place of service as "the place where your deep gladness meets the world's deep need."[5]

Elaborating on Buechner's words, Parker Palmer added in *Let Your Life Speak*:

> Buechner's definition starts with the self and moves toward the needs of the world: it begins, wisely, where vocation begins—not in what the world needs (which is everything), but in the nature of the human self, in what

brings the self joy, the deep joy of knowing that we are
here on earth to be the gifts that God created.[6]

This challenges us with the task of discovering our gifts and genuine interests, assessing the needs around us, and finding the
intersection where they can meet.

"I'm a frustrated actress," admitted Veronica, "so I found a
kindergarten teacher who needed a volunteer to read to the kids
once a week. Those kids got more than they bargained for," she
chuckled. "They not only heard the words, but they heard them
with all the dramatic flair this old granny could muster! It was a
win-win."

"We all have something important to give," insisted Wayne,
"whether we're manning a phone bank or stuffing envelopes or
teaching calculus. We can't wait for the activity to land on our
doorstep or pray that God will miraculously provide it for us. Not
that things don't sometimes happen that way, but I think we have
to do our part in the process of building a life that matters."

Time and talent are valuable commodities indeed, but we
need to use them thoughtfully. In the context of aging, time can
become friend instead of foe.

The Many Faces of Freedom

Freedom was cited more often than any other gift of later life.
However, like the gift of time, freedom is a double-edged sword.
It carries its own paradoxical meaning when deciding what to do
with it:

The good news is you don't have to ask anyone.

The bad news is you don't have to ask anyone.

Freedom means that you have the responsibility for making
the decision yourself. It can be both intoxicating and frightening.
"To be able to blame others for making poor choices or creating
unpleasant circumstances is a comfortable cushion—it means it
isn't my fault," reported Suzanne. "I realize my son and his family are in a difficult situation and want us to help by moving in

with them. We plan to help, but we don't want to completely relinquish the freedom we've found in this life stage."

"There's nothing quite as exhilarating as freedom of choice," asserted Anthony. "I think it's necessary for good mental health. But there's a risk involved: it might not turn out like you thought. So what? Being willing to fall flat on your face or to change your mind in midstream is life-giving and challenging—like walking a tightrope without falling off. Safety and security are poor substitutes for freedom to choose, especially in later life. I'm connecting with my freedom to make mistakes."

Freedom from the constraints of younger years—family demands, society's expectations, responsibility for child rearing—made Madge and Clyde consider what it meant to have more choices. "I'm free to lighten up on my own self-judgment," Madge said as she reached for another chocolate brownie. "I'm making no more apologies about gray hair or extra pounds or eating dessert first. I'd rather have this freedom than a flat belly, anyway."

Clyde had this thoughtful response about the power of choice: "We want to take responsibility for this last stage of our lives, because we do have a choice. We can choose to bellyache over the way the kids treat us or how inattentive the grandchildren are or blather endlessly about our aches and pains—or we can behave like grown-ups and milk the nectar out of this stage of life for all it's worth. Most of us have harvested some rich truths during the years, and even if the younger set doesn't want to hear the intelligent fruit of our experience, we can at least apply the wisdom to ourselves."

Fran was eager to use the gift of freedom to explore unlived parts of herself. "Even though I've been extremely active, surrounded by five children and all the baggage that brings, I've always wondered what it would be like to feed my introverted side. So I've signed up for a weeklong silent retreat at a monastery. There's a part of me that wants to explore what it would feel like to experience the belovedness of a child of God rather than the work ethic of a servant."

For many of us, it helps to imagine this newfound freedom as standing before a delicious buffet of choices. We can be paralyzed with the options before us. It's best to take a bite of this or that until we find something that "tastes good." Then we can choose a larger portion or an entire plateful.

This kind of freedom may seem to run counter to the religious mandate that most of us grew up with—that of obedience. Obedience as we have defined it through the years contains an aura of coercion, doing things because we must, we're supposed to, they expect us to, we have to or else. True freedom, however, takes us beyond obedience to genuine choice from the heart. We often obey with gritted teeth, but we choose with a smile.

Looking Inside

1. Can you think of a situation in which you refrain from being your true self? Explore your motives—to please others? To be acceptable to others? To be in "compliance" with religious dogma? To be loved?

2. What do you consider "playing"? When is the last time you had a genuine belly laugh? How often do you break into a smile?

3. When faced with a negative situation, do you rush to the worst-case scenario? Think of ways you can move toward gratitude and "tone your gratitude muscle."

4. What percentage of your attention is present in the moment? Is your focus on the past? On the future?

5. What choices are you making with the liberation of later years? How are you choosing to invest your time?

6. How are your choices making a difference in your community? In the world?

Surprising Wisdom

So teach us to count our days, that we may gain a wise heart.

PSALMS 90:12

Does not wisdom call out? Does not understanding raise her voice?

PROVERBS 8:1

A ctor Alan Alda is credited with saying that it's better to be wise than smart. I caught the full significance of that statement during the interviews for this book, for indeed wisdom and intelligence are not the same.

Wisdom is defined as knowledge understood and applied. Take that definition apart and elaborate a bit, and it becomes knowledge (perceived in the head), understood (evident in our experience), and applied (lived out in existence). In other words, something that moves from the head to the heart and then to the hands. The journey of wisdom starts with listening to life's experiences, learning the lessons they offer, and developing a deeper understanding of what's true and important.

The process of becoming wise can also be viewed as divine alchemy—taking the "straw" of life (the rough, raw, unrefined stuff) and spinning it into pure gold. Or, to follow the words of the psalmist, we "count" our days not numerically, but by squeezing out the distilled wisdom from our accumulated life experience. These are the gold nuggets that we bequeath to others.

Kathryn, too, described wisdom as an alchemical process. "In my mind, we need divine help to achieve true wisdom about anything," she declared. "It's as if we stir up the stuff of our lives, mix it with lots of grace and forgiveness, and allow God to help us turn it into gold. Then it's our task to embody it and pass it on."

Probably the most humorous take on the matter of wisdom came from a jolly gentleman with a quick quip for almost any subject. Ned leaned forward with a grin and said, "Knowledge is knowing that a tomato is a fruit; wisdom is not putting it in a fruit salad."

Most seniors I interviewed, however, were dead serious about the winnowed wisdom they were eager to pass on. So here goes.

Living through Loss

"Unless you learn to deal with loss, you'll have a pretty miserable later life," testified Earl. "When Ginger died, I was overwhelmed with what I had lost—my companion, my friend, my life partner—not to mention our way of life as a couple. But finally I didn't want to exist in the devastation any longer, and I shifted my focus."

I asked Earl how he did it, and he was very specific. "Rather than focusing on the losses that resulted from her death, I started thinking about the gains I experienced from her life—our three children and eight grandchildren, the beautiful sofa she chose for the living room, her support that made me a better man. 'Grateful and sad' feel better to me than 'bitter and sad.' As a friend told me, 'Grief teaches us lessons that joy can never know.'"

Another widower agreed. A man of few words, Woodrow had a will of iron. "Tears happen," he stated. "I don't mean to make light of it, but a person has to endure, grieve, then move on. I want to be *alive* while I'm still alive."

Look at any data on aging well and you'll find a recurrent common denominator that ranks well ahead of eating carrots and walking a mile a day—and that's the ability to adapt to loss. The later years offer unexpected layers of loss that can challenge even the most optimistic among us. When confronted with the concept of loss, our minds usually shift to the funeral of a loved one or a moving van headed from the family home to a retirement facility. Those are powerful losses indeed, but Veronica found that it was more than that.

"At first, I thought of letting go in terms of what I could see with my eyes—my husband, my home, a favorite painting. I hadn't considered the intangible things—my youth, my vigor, my independence—those deeper currents caught me by surprise. Dealing with loss needs to become a healthy habit of letting go, not a onetime fix."

Helen made the distinction between losses that happen to us and things we wisely choose to lose. "I can't do anything about death and taxes," she reported, "but I've found that there are some things that I *need* to lose!" Here is her working list of intentional goodbyes, which she revises daily:

- Habit of complaining
- Resentment toward a family member
- Tendency to judge
- Feeling of uselessness
- Needless worry

Many respondents pointed out the freedom each of us has to respond to losses with wisdom. Faye summed up her opinions with a smile: "After all, what does responsibility for our choices really mean? Pure and simple, it's our ability to respond in positive ways. Let me put it this way: I may lose my waistline, but I don't want to lose my sense of humor about it."

When columnist Ellen Goodman wrote about the losses involved in retirement, she offered these wise comments:

> There's a trick to the Graceful Exit. It begins with the vision to recognize when a job, a life stage, a relationship is over—and to let go. It means leaving what's over without denying its validity or its past importance in our lives…. It involves a sense of future, a belief that every exit line is an entry, that we are moving on rather than out…. The trick of retiring well may be the trick of living well. It's hard to recognize that life isn't a holding action, but a process. It's hard to learn that we don't leave the best parts of ourselves behind, back in the dugout or the office. We own what we learned back there. The experiences and the growth are grafted onto our lives. And when we exit, we can take ourselves along—quite gracefully.[1]

Ultimately, everything in our lives is subject to loss—health, home, family, friends—and there is profound wisdom in having the courage to discover what's left when everything observable is taken away. The patterns of loss and gain are embedded in every layer of our lives, even in the natural act of breathing as we take in air, then release it.

- We have to let go of one breath before we can breathe in another one. Our physical health depends on it.
- We have to let go of a negative thought before a positive thought can take its place. Our mental health depends on it.

The "knots and tangles" of loss in later life make weavers of us all as we create new patterns in our days and our spirits. One senior, a weaver herself, offered this insight: the very Love that created these complex lives of ours is, in fact, the Master Weaver.

Say It Now and Do It Now

Signs on church marquees are usually more pithy than profound, but I spotted one recently that is worth mentioning: "Aspire to inspire before you expire." In other words, don't procrastinate when words need to be spoken.

Many a person at life's end is eager to tell family members how dearly they are loved and valued, even if they've always been reticent about expressing feelings. Regret at not having spoken words of affection and approval can cloud our later lives, but it's never too late to start speaking.

Virginia decided not to waste another minute. "I don't let a day pass without telling my spouse that I love him," she declared. "If my grandson completes a stack of Lego blocks, I say, 'Good job—you'll be an engineer someday!' I even cornered my pastor to tell him how his sermons had enriched my spiritual life. What am I waiting for? I need to say those things while I still have breath!"

Perry expanded his circle of goodwill beyond his family group. "Have you noticed that almost every working person wears a name badge? I've started calling everyone by name whom I possibly can; it makes them feel as if they are truly *seen*."

"The grocery store is a great place to practice words of encouragement," offered Belle. "It provides a kind of laboratory in unscripted human behavior. Instead of merely thinking that the checkout clerk is long-suffering, I might say, 'Sally, you're a patient woman; you never get ruffled!' Or, instead of taking the bagger for granted, I say, 'Charlie, thanks for putting all the frozen foods in the same bag!' Or if the person behind my full basket of groceries has only two items, I invite her to go ahead of me."

When a TV technician patiently hooked up her cable service and instructed her in its use, Wanda noted his name and called his supervisor to report his outstanding service. "I don't want to someday have regrets about all the things I should have said or meant to say, but was too lazy to do it," she revealed.

This goes for our deeds as well as our words. "'I'll do it later' needs to be replaced by 'I'll do it *now*,'" suggested Molly, a hospice volunteer. "I've had the privilege of sitting with quite a number of dying folks, and none of them wished they had spent more time at the office," she disclosed. "Sometimes they regret that they lived the life others expected of them, rather than the life they wanted to live. They talk about things they wish they had done and risks they wish they had taken."

In my work as a spiritual director, I've heard many versions of the sentiments, "What shall I do *now*? What is God's purpose for me? I've prayed and prayed to be shown what to do with my life, and I'm still waiting." The dictates of most major religious traditions center around loving God and loving our neighbors. What if *that is* our purpose? Often, we are searching for a lofty, high-profile task when what we are called to do is lift the spirits of the person right in front of us.

These words of an anonymous writer underline the urgency of action:

> *First, I was dying to finish my high school and start college;*
> *And then I was dying to finish college and start working;*
> *Then I was dying to marry and have children;*
> *And then I was dying for my children to grow old enough*
> *So I could go back to work.*
> *But then I was dying to retire;*
> *And now I am dying …*
> *And suddenly I realized I forgot to live.*

Clearing the Clutter

- "We have too much *stuff*. Just taking care of it all is eating up our time and money."
- "I feel this powerful need to simplify my life—you know, pare things down."
- "That old cliché 'You can't take it with you' takes on a stark reality as you age—makes you want to get rid of things."
- "As I get older and wiser, I feel a need to *have* less and *do* less."

The seniors I spoke with offered astute advice about cluttered houses, cluttered schedules, cluttered minds, and cluttered spirits. Their prevailing wisdom was: simplify, simplify, simplify.

"I thought cleaning out the garage was going to start a third world war," confided Harold. "I'm a notorious neatnik, and Charlene is a pack rat—never throws away anything. We finally reached a truce when we agreed on our list of decision questions."

Their discernment process for disposing of items is worth sharing:

- Do I love it?
- Do I need it to be happy?
- Does it support who I am now in my life?
- Does it spark pleasant memories?
- Does it need to be repaired, and am I willing to do so *now?*
- If it's time to let it go, does it belong in the sell pile, the give-away pile, or the trash pile?
- Who in my community might need this?

Simplifying your schedule carried its own set of considerations. Alice offered, "Now that I'm wiser, I pause before saying yes to anything—even a dinner invitation. I ask myself if I really want to go or if I'm going because I think I ought to. I even try to be honest about whether I can be myself with this particular group of people. I don't want to pretend anymore."

Decluttering your time can also mean facing our culture's addiction to busyness. "As I began to question my motives in choosing how to spend my time, I stumbled on an unexpected part of myself," confessed Maria. "I had bought society's measure of worth—hook, line, and sinker. Being busy had become a way of life for me, something that gave me a hidden degree of pride. I discovered that I was getting an unconscious psychological pay-off—a way of enhancing my own importance, I guess. I had an ego investment in appearing to be energetic and active—even if it no longer reflected what I wanted or needed. After all, folks don't usually reward you for staring out the window or sometimes slowing down to a crawl."

George offered a great quip on the subject of busyness: "Man begins to cut his wisdom teeth the first time he bites off more than he can chew. Something has to go. Better to be calm and focused on a few important things than breathless and confused about a lot of things."

The inner guidance to simplify our lives runs smack into the cultural message that says "produce and possess." It's worth shining a light on our motives to see if we've bought into that message. Do we use those twin imperatives—produce and possess—as a measuring stick for ourselves and for others? The wisdom of later life calls us to value who we are more than what we do or have.

Addressing a cluttered mind, however, requires some serious thought management. A mind full of racing thoughts robs us of the serenity that produces peace and stability. "I've learned to slow down my mind, and it's the best thing that ever happened to me," reported Mark. "Meditation allows the mind to do less, not more. I think it makes room for wisdom. Otherwise, we crowd it out with our own mindless chatter."

"It's quite a responsibility to be the gatekeeper of our own thoughts, but that's what we are," insisted Kitty. "I watch what I let into my inner sanctuary—not simply pleasant thoughts, but meaningful thoughts. If I'm wrestling with troublesome thoughts, I make sure it's worth it. No need to repeat upsetting stuff in your head if you aren't going to act on it."

These comments echo the wise words of spiritual teacher Eckhart Tolle, "The primary cause of unhappiness is never the situation but your thoughts about it."[2] Our thoughts can direct us toward magic or misery. If we consider thought as a symphony conductor in the psyche, do we want Mozart or a mindless melody?

A cluttered spirit calls for a deepening focus on your relationship with the Holy, a movement toward inner spaciousness. Chester pointed out the necessity of learning to "Be still and know that I am God" (Psalms 46:10). "I had never learned to actually be still," he recounted. "I was more of a doer. I had associated spiritual growth with reading another book or tackling another worthy project or learning from a spiritual leader. But those external influences alone can continue to clutter the spirit. I had to develop the habit of being still before God—opening up the interior space with no expectations."

All in all, these seniors saw a correlation between outer clutter and inner confusion. Identifying their own patterns of clutter nudged them toward simplicity in all its forms.

As Simple as a Smile

Ninety-eight-year-old Mary has a fascinating early-morning routine. Still living independently in a retirement-home apartment, she starts her day with the following self-message: "This is a good day; it's all I have. Who needs what I have to offer? I'll give to others whatever I can, even it it's simply a smile." Then with a twinkle in her eye, she adds, "Besides, I've always been told that a smile is an inexpensive way to improve your looks!"

Later in the interview, I asked her what she had learned about herself during the aging process. "I've always been an optimist," she declared, "but I didn't realize how important that trait would be in these later years. Without a positive outlook on life, it's hard to deal with all the challenges."

The seniors who appeared to be thriving, rather than merely surviving, shared another significant common denominator. They found some way to give of themselves on a regular basis. Usually, their charitable acts were evidenced in tiny gestures, not necessarily grand projects. Repeating Mary's words, it could be "as simple as a smile."

Ray vowed to do at least one unrewarded act of kindness each day. "It doesn't have to be much," he insisted. "Letting someone into a traffic lane or stopping for a person to cross the street—just doing something for someone who can't pay you back. Recently, I was leaving a restaurant and noticed the young man busily busing the tables. I knew he was the low man on the tipping chain, so I went over to him, told him what a great job he was doing, and pressed a five-dollar bill into his hand. He was so startled that he hugged me, right on the spot!"

Al spoke about putting the brakes on his opinions as part of his effort to be kind. "I have mighty strong views on just about everything," he laughed, "but I've learned that it's more important to be kind than right, to be caring rather than convincing. I don't have to win the argument anymore."

He offered a simple quiz to help prove his point. (No pen and paper needed.)

1. Name the five wealthiest people in the world.
2. Name the last five Heisman trophy winners.
3. Name the last winner of the Miss America contest.
4. Name two recent winners of the Nobel or Pulitzer Prize.
5. Name the last two Academy Award winners for best actor.

These are the headliners of yesterday and first-rate achievers, the best in their fields. But the applause dies, awards tarnish. Accolades and certificates are buried with their owners. Now answer these:

1. List three teachers who aided your journey through school.
2. Name three friends who helped you through a difficult time.
3. Name five people who taught you something worthwhile.
4. Think of three people who made you feel appreciated.
5. Think of five folks you enjoy spending time with.
6. Name three heroes whose stories have inspired you.

The lesson is obvious. The people who make a difference in your life aren't the ones with the most credentials, the most money, or the most awards. They're the ones who *care.*

Celeste considered these random gestures in a more cosmic context. "I don't believe any kindness is ever wasted," she asserted, "no matter how insignificant it seems. Every loving act is like a drop in the ocean of spiritual evolution on this planet. Just because we don't understand how that works doesn't mean it isn't so. Charity plays a part in some mysterious, mystical way. That goes for our loving thoughts and prayers, too. Even if I'm lying flat on my back, I can offer a prayer and know that somehow, some way, it matters."

This puzzling power of blessing is the subject of a beautiful poem by Steve Garnaas-Holmes. Here are excerpts from his work:

> *I carry my secret power through this world,*
> *Hidden, so that you will not see it....*
> *It never tires or errs or fails;*
> *It prevails in public or in secret,*
> *With a single one or a whole clan.*
> *It does not protect me or hand me success,*
> *But it always triumphs, always lives,*
> *Though often I will suffer for it, but only a bit....*
> *It streams from my heart to all whom I meet,*
> *But they seldom know it was me,*
> *Since it takes effect so slowly.*
> *I walk through the market, I read the paper,*
> *I watch the dryer repairman, the grocery clerk,*
> *People who drive, who walk, who yell at me,*
> *Secretly radiating the gift that I have been given,*
> *Seldom speaking of it, but letting it flow:*
> *"Blessing." "Blessing." "Blessing."*[3]

Learn to Receive

"I've been a *giver* all my life," professed Edith, "and learning to receive is going against the grain for me. In recovering from this broken hip, I've become a real grouch because I'm unable to do things for myself."

Roger's moment of challenge came when he heard himself whining (for the umpteenth time), "I used to be able to put up the rooftop Christmas lights with no problem, but look at me now. I'm absolutely useless!" He realized that his wounded pride was turning him into an irritating martyr. Though he wanted to be more gracious, the truth was he regarded asking for help as a sign of weakness—even moral failure.

Requesting and receiving assistance from others can be a bitter pill as age requires it with increasing urgency. It also begs the question "Who am I now that I can't do what I used to do?" Isn't it possible that acknowledging and accepting our dependence on others can be a show of strength, rather than weakness?

Corinne became aware of the need to shift her focus without becoming a shrew, but she had to overcome her unconscious sense of entitlement. "Inside, I was having a temper tantrum, wondering why I was having to go through this unexpected (and *undeserved*, I thought) heart condition. Finally, it dawned on me that everyone had struggles of his or her own, and this diminishment wasn't happening to me alone. Who doesn't go through these things? It's just life." Then she added with a laugh, "I guess I thought that if I behaved myself and followed the health rules, the gods would make an exception in my case. Talk about arrogance."

Joan Chittister made these insightful comments:

> Life, everybody's life, is an excursion from dark to light, from contradiction to hope, from one circumstance and stage to another—all of them meant to stretch us to the fullness of ourselves and to the real meaning of what it is to be fully alive.... As a result, it is the way we deal with the dark and difficult moments that makes all the difference as to how they affect us in the long run.... Life, in the end, is really about coming to live it deeply, coming to live it well, beginning to live it as a spiritual experience rather than as a perpetual burden or an eternal Disneyland.[4]

Sam honored his physical decline by using it as a spiritual discipline. "I used to complain that my body was betraying me. Then I realized that my body was doing exactly what it was supposed to do—start wearing out. Acceptance of that fact without bitterness has become my spiritual exercise."

"If you think life should be trouble-free, and yours isn't, you're fighting a losing battle," contributed Terry. "If you're always in a state of discontent, reveling in what's wrong with you or what's missing from your life, you're probably not thinking about what's good about it. The task is to change the way you think. I ask myself three questions at the end of the day: What am I thankful for today? How did I serve others today? And what am I satisfied about today? You can always come up with something."

Reaching some level of acceptance about your condition seemed to be a prerequisite for the freedom to receive help graciously. "Once I stopped behaving like such a victim, I was able to shift from 'Why can't I do that?' to 'What can I still do?'" asserted Valerie. "Though I was non-ambulatory for a while, I could still plan meals and make grocery lists. Plus, I could ask clearly for what I needed instead of waiting for folks to figure it out. My friends genuinely wanted to help, but I needed to help them help me. So, if they were coming over to visit and asked if they could bring something, I would say, 'Would you mind picking up a carton of eggs and a pound of coffee?' They were delighted to do it, of course, and seemed to appreciate my directness. I imagine they liked that better than my whining!" she said with a chuckle.

Valerie had thoughtfully put herself in the shoes of her friends. She preferred that they be clear with her about their needs, so she decided to give that same gift of directness to them. "One other thing about learning to receive," she included. "It's a golden opportunity to get in touch with a little humility and a lot of gratitude. I changed from making constant apologies for my dependence to saying constant thank-yous for the support others offered. I even occasionally asked someone to rub lotion on my sore back."

The receptive posture of later life need not mean that our days of giving are over. The truth is, however, that we can't give away what we don't possess, and we can't give out of an empty cup. Finding ways to be open to the love of God refills our reservoir of grace so that we can leave a legacy of love and service. A simple practice of regular receiving is as close as our breath:

Breathing in, imagine you are being filled with divine love and healing.

Breathing out, visualize that unbounded sacred energy moving out to others.

What could be easier? We can always give a kind word, a bit of encouragement, a grateful hug, a warm smile, or (when energy permits) a pot of chicken soup.

Fan the Brightest Flame

The glory of God is a (person) fully alive.
IRENAEUS

"The best way to feel really alive in later life is to find out what lights your fire, and fan that flame," suggested Clarence. "Of course, that means that you also need to discover what douses that flame."

Perennial wisdom from many sources affirms his suggestion.

- "Follow your bliss." (Joseph Campbell)
- "Energy flows where attention goes." (Serge Kahili King)
- "Whatever is true, whatever is noble, whatever is right, whatever is pure, whatever is lovely, whatever is admirable—if anything is excellent or praiseworthy—think about such things." (Philippians 4:8)
- "For where your treasure is, there your heart will be also." (Matthew 6:21)
- "Ask not what the world needs. Ask what makes you come alive ... then go do it. Because what the world needs are people who have come alive." (Howard Thurman)

Identifying what lights our fire calls for paying close attention to the specific things that tend to enliven us—noticing when our curiosity is aroused, when we lose track of time, when we're thoroughly present to the moment, or when we feel lighthearted. (In chapter 2, I offered additional questions designed to uncover those feelings on page 46).

When we live only from our acquired skills—the things we have learned how to do—we can easily become exhausted. When we live from our gifts and passions, however, we become energized, both physically and emotionally. Put another way, it can be the difference between surviving and thriving at any stage of our life. This wise group of seniors had specific suggestions about which flames to fan.

Fan the Flame of Curiosity

A declining zest for life can sometimes occur by default: we simply fail to notice and nurture the sparks of curiosity that arise naturally. Untended, that flame eventually sputters out.

"I had always wanted to know more about China—all the Asian countries, in fact—but I never acted on it," remembered Howard. "I finally gave myself a swift kick in the pants and enrolled in a free audit course at the local university. Of course, I had to set my objections aside—Where will I park? Will the undergrads treat me like an old geezer? Will I be able to keep up intellectually? But it ignited something inside me, and it was well worth the effort. I felt years younger, and it kept my brain cells busy."

Howard and others described an internal rocket boost of energy when doing something new, risky, or adventurous. Nora related an experience with her two grandsons on a trip to Disneyworld. "They were pestering me to get on those crazy rides with them, and I ran out of excuses. When I got in line for the Tower of Terror, my knees were knocking. I lived through it, though, and the look of affirmation on their faces made me feel pretty spunky for a seventy-year-old. But I drew the line at that upside-down roller coaster!"

I recalled the words of a hospice worker, who reported that the greatest regrets of those at the end of life were risks not taken, adventures not pursued, and curiosity unsatisfied. In the words of Mark Twain, "Twenty years from now, you'll be more disappointed by the things you didn't do than by the things you did do." Moreover, studies show that the nature of the activity doesn't matter as much as the attention with which you engage in it. Whether it is digging in the garden, knitting a sweater, cooking a stew, standing over a putt, or hiking a trail, enthusiasm fans the flame.

Fan the Flame of Optimism

"There is no such thing as an idle thought," offered Lisa. "Our thoughts shape our reality, so it's wise to monitor your mind. Science is telling us that thoughts produce feelings; feelings produce emotions; emotions produce action; action produces experience."

Our culture seems much more obsessed with what we feed our bodies than what we feed our minds. How many calories? How much fiber? Did we get our five servings of fruits and veggies today? But our minds take "bites" from a huge buffet of offerings—violent movies, ridiculous TV sitcoms, trashy novels, idle gossip—all junk food for the brain. To retain any measure of hope and optimism, we must become aware of our own complicity in this junk-food diet.

Kurt was struggling to find the balance between reality and hope. "I don't want to ignore the troubles and tragedies in the world, but I try to balance thoughts about what's right with the world with what's wrong with it."

Fan the Flame of Friends and Family

Nothing brings quite as much zest to life as nourishing relationships. Conversely, nothing douses that lively flame more drastically than depleting relationships. "Sometimes we stay with folks who drain the sap out of our souls, just because we don't stop and think about what we're doing," Shirley said with exasperation. "It isn't rocket science; it's simple cause and effect."

Usually, it's only a matter of noticing what a relationship is doing to us. Does it bring out the best in me? Do I feel better or worse when I talk to her on the phone? Do I feel smothered by him? Do I feel safe and accepted? We can make wise choices about those with whom we spend most of our time. Even if troublesome folks live in the house with us, we're not trapped. We can choose to confront the things that are draining us and alter the nature of the relationship.

But we can't change the toxic atmosphere unless we have the courage to become aware of it and *act*. The solution to this dilemma is normally a matter of spending less time with that person or group or relating to them with clearer boundaries.

Gigi chimed in with yet more probing questions. "Does it seem as if the air has been sucked out of the room when you're with that group? Are you bored or stimulated? Do your burdens feel lighter or heavier? Do you feel hopeful or discouraged? Relaxed or uptight? Smiling or frowning? Validated or diminished? All those reactions tell you something about what gives you life and what doesn't."

Fan the Flame of Your Spiritual Life

"I don't go to church much anymore," admitted Diane. "I get bored. Besides, I don't like the style of music at my church."

Diane began to notice the kinds of music and worship environments that enhanced her ability to connect with the Holy. She explored everything from ancient chants to contemporary compositions until she found the liturgical and musical styles that brought her closer to God. Then she explored a variety of personal prayer practices and spiritual disciplines that revived her sagging spirit.

Annette wasn't much of a meditator and was looking for a spiritual practice that would enrich her soul. She found just what she was looking for in Sybil MacBeth's book *Praying in Color.*[5] The technique requires no proven artistic ability, merely a willingness to pick up some brightly colored pens and start doodling as you pray. As her body participated in the prayer and the colors stimulated her imagination, Annette found an unusual way to feed her spirit.

The key to a livelier life in the later years is to find the activities, behaviors, and relationships that are enriching to you and others, and do more of them. Or, as a horse-loving friend of mine advises, "Climb on a great horse, then take it at a gallop!"

One Who Never Leaves You

Neither death nor life, neither angels nor demons, neither the present nor the future, nor any powers, neither height nor depth, nor anything else in all creation, will be able to separate us from the love of God.

ROMANS 8:38, 39

This foundation is the gift that has always been ours. From the cradle to the grave, from seven to seventy, it follows us and fuels our aliveness. This Love is the solid gold in the golden years.

Everything you can imagine is subject to loss—your house, your job, your health, your friends and family—even your own life. Loved ones can surround you. They can put their hand in your hand, but they can't go with you.

As a person who is prone to planning, I've already chosen the music for my own funeral. Ironically, the hymn that tops my list is an old composition from the early 1900s that reflects this sentiment:

O Love that wilt not let me go,
I rest my weary soul in thee;
I give thee back the life I owe,
That in thine ocean depths, its flow
May richer, fuller be.

O Light that followest all my way,
I yield my flickering torch to thee;
My heart restores its borrowed ray,
That in thy sunshine's blaze, its day
May brighter, fairer be.[6]

I'm not trying to end this book with tragedy, but rather with truth. Later life is the time when we get in touch with the big picture, the core meaning, the ultimate reality. It's a time to change and grow from within, because lasting joy is an inside job.

"I feel a part of something larger than myself," reflected Marie, "something bigger than my limited little world, part of the whole creation." Whether we call this Something the Collective Unconscious, the Luminous Web, the Ground of All Being, the Source of All That Is, or the Mind of God, the truth is that we are all part of it. Separation is not possible.

The metaphor of the wave and the water can guide us through this mystery. Remember that an individual wave begins and ends, but at the same time, it is made of water, which has no beginning or ending. If we imagine the wave as the natural changing conditions of old age, we can understand the water as that part of us that doesn't age or alter. However, knowledge about this "living water" and experience of it are two different things.

Joan Chittister writes, "It's easy to keep a religious checklist and call that a religious life. It is far more difficult to become a spiritual person for whom life is more an adventure in spiritual growth and wisdom than it is a series of setbacks, an endless list of woes. God does not create us to tease our appetites and test our endurance. God creates us to enable us to see the Face of God in every dimension of life."[7]

This includes the final dimension also—our last years and our transition from this life to the next. We have the opportunity to treat these days like the treasures they are, cherishing one day at a time. The psalmist reminded us that "this is the day the Lord has made," not yesterday is the day, or tomorrow is the day. No, it says *this* is the day. Divine Presence is always here—in both the tough and the tender moments.

As human beings we want to hedge our bets, know what's coming next so we can prepare for it. But no one has a crystal ball. In fact, preoccupation with the future distracts us from the present, and we're likely to miss the twists and turns of the unexpected.

We won't find God by gazing into heaven or sticking our heads in the clouds, but by attending to the holy in our lives, our relationships, and our compassion. Only then can we welcome the spiritual surprises of later life. Only then can we leave a legacy of Love.

Epilogue

As I was completing the final chapter of this book, I found myself on the road to Savannah, Tennessee, to be with my beloved aunt in her final chapter. It was Christmas week, and I had hospice conversations, as well as grandchildren and nativity scenes, swirling in my head at the same time. It felt as if the Christ child, Santa Claus, and the Grim Reaper were all knocking at the door. I wanted to be able to greet those disparate guests with hospitality.

How typical of later life, as we are repeatedly presented with experiential grist for the mill, where sadness and joy are wrapped up together, where the circle of life demands that we honor the dying and care for the living.

Perhaps that's the essence of what I've tried to say in this book. This life stage is like every other stage—it's a mixed bag, full of surprises. When we give ourselves to the richness of that mixture, we are shaped into something whole: real live human beings.

Aunt Irene was a strong, hopeful woman, who was just a few days shy of her ninety-ninth birthday. For me, she embodied the words of writer Albert Camus: "In the midst of winter, I found in me an invincible summer." Thank God, that invincible summer is in every one of us, too.

Acknowledgments

No one births a book alone. It "takes a village" of people who believe in the project and are willing to devote hours to it with no hope of reward (well, maybe a hug and a free book!).

My village includes a quintet of readers, scattered from Ohio to Mississippi and from Maryland to Memphis. They pored over words, concepts, and (sometimes) debatable theology to help turn out a solid text.

Thanks to Gloria Folk for her skeptical eyes and willingness to ask the hard questions; to Mary Ellen Culp for her unique responses of the emotions as well as of the intellect; to Craig Jordan for his keen professorial mind combined with a servant heart; to my sister Anita, an incredibly creative wordsmith; and to Wayne Young, minister, physician, and friend for his obsession with good grammar, medical accuracy, and grounded theology. Your contributions were like silver spokes on a wheel, all aimed at the same shining central goal—a worthwhile manuscript.

Special thanks to the talented team at SkyLight Paths. Your editing, copyediting, designing, and publishing skills were far above my pay grade. You made my dream happen. And I even grew to love the two chickens on the cover.

Of course, we would have had little to work with without the candid comments of the dozens of seniors who agreed to my interviews. You allowed me to pry into your private thoughts and hidden anxieties with my nosy questions. The wise and risky responses you offered are the heart and soul of this book. I am so thankful to all of you that I wish I could set music to my gratitude and sing it in Carnegie Hall.

Linda Douty
Memphis, Tennessee

Notes

1. Opening to Surprise

1. Cynthia Bourgeault, *The Wisdom Way of Knowing* (San Francisco: Jossey-Bass, 2003), 74–75.
2. Quoted in Joan Chittister, *The Gift of Years* (New York: Bluebridge Books, 2008), 197.
3. Ellen Goodman, "Letting Go, and Looking Ahead," *Boston Globe*, January 1, 2010.
4. Tom Brokaw, commencement address, Emory University, Atlanta, Ga., May 16, 2005.
5. John Dainith and Anne Stibbs, eds., *Bloomsbury Treasury of Quotations* (London: Bloomsbury, 1994), 13.
6. Judy Sorum Brown, *The Sea Accepts All Rivers & Other Poems* (Alexandria, Va.: Miles River Press, 2000), 17.
7. David Steindl-Rast, "A Good Day," video clip, www.gratefulness.org/brotherdavid/a-good-day.htm.
8. Jack Riemer, "Perlman Makes His Music—The Hard Way," *Houston Chronicle*, November 18, 1995.
9. Pierre Teilhard de Chardin, *The Phenomenon of Man* (New York: Harper, 1959), 169.

2. Surprises of the Self

1. Mark Nepo, *The Book of Awakening* (York Beach, Maine: Conari Press, 2000), 3.
2. Steve Garnaas-Holmes, "Realize the Moment," *Unfolding Light* (blog), August 13, 2000, http://unfolding-light.blogspot.com.
3. James Hollis, *Finding Meaning in the Second Half of Life* (New York: Gotham Books, 2005), 31, 34.
4. Parker Palmer, *A Hidden Wholeness* (San Francisco: Jossey-Bass, 2005), 58.
5. Kathleen Norris, *Acedia & Me* (New York: Riverhead Books, 2008), 2–3.
6. Linda Douty, *How Can I Let Go If I Don't Know I'm Holding On?* (Harrisburg, Penn.: Morehouse Press, 2005), 36–37.
7. Steve Garnaas-Holmes, "What Do You Pay Attention To?" *Unfolding Light* (blog), August 16, 2010, http://unfolding-light.blogspot.com.

8. Serge Kahili King, *Urban Shaman* (New York: Fireside / Simon & Schuster, 1990), 171.

9. Linda Douty, "What If It Hadn't Rained?" in *Compass Club Writers Memphis Collection* (Nashville, Tenn.: Cold Tree Press, 2007), 123–124.

10. Dawna Markova, *I Will Not Die an Unlived Life* (Boston: Conari Press, 2000), 1.

3. Surprises of the Body

1. Judith Viorst, *Necessary Losses* (New York: Simon & Schuster, 1986), 269.

2. Barbara Brown Taylor, *An Altar in the World* (New York: HarperCollins, 2009), 157.

3. Ibid., 172.

4. Ibid., 158.

5. Douty, *How Can I Let Go*, 32.

6. Taylor, *An Altar in the World*, 159.

7. Julian of Norwich, *Revelations of Divine Love*, trans. Elizabeth Spearing (New York: Penguin, 1998), 22.

8. Eknath Easwaran, *Words to Live By* (Tomales, Calif.: Nilgiri Press, 1999), 284.

9. Linda Douty, "It-Is-As-It-Is Prayer," in *Praying in the Messiness of Life* (Nashville, Tenn.: Upper Room Books, 2011), 84.

4. Surprises in Relationships

1. Oriah Mountain Dreamer, *The Invitation* (San Francisco: HarperOne, 1999), 1.

2. Robert Benson, personal correspondence with author.

3. Douty, *How Can I Let Go*, 142.

4. Steve Garnaas-Holmes, "Water into Wine," *Unfolding Light* (blog), January 11, 2010, http://unfolding-light.blogspot.com.

5. Palmer, *A Hidden Wholeness*, 55.

5. Surprises of the Sacred

1. Douty, *Praying in the Messiness of Life*, 84.

2. Robert Morris, "Listening for the Voice," *Weavings: A Journal of the Christian Spiritual Life* 25, no. 3 (August 2010): 10–11. www.weavings.org.

3. Marjorie Thompson, "The Pathway and the Pilgrimage" (address, Academy for Spiritual Formation, Nashville, Tenn., October 16–22, 2010).

4. See Douty, *Praying in the Messiness of Life* for dozens of alternative prayer forms listed and described in this text.

5. For further ideas, see Douty, *How Can I Let Go*, 65–67, or Cynthia Bourgeault, *Centering Prayer and Inner Awakening* (Cambridge, Mass.: Cowley, 2004), an excellent source for information on silent prayer.

6. Surprising Challenges

1. Sue Monk Kidd, *Firstlight* (New York: Guideposts Books, 2006), 90.
2. Flora Wuellner, "When the Stars Begin to Fall," *Weavings: A Journal of the Christian Spiritual Life* 25, no. 4 (November 2010): 4, 42. www.weavings.org.
3. Frederick Buechner, *Wishful Thinking* (New York: HarperSanFrancisco, 1973), 2.
4. Chittister, *The Gift of Years*, 3.
5. Douty, *How Can I Let Go*, 92.
6. Steve Garnaas-Holmes, "Repent," *Unfolding Light* (blog), March 3, 2010, http://unfolding-light.blogspot.com.

7. Surprising Gifts

1. Henri Nouwen, "All Is Grace," *Weavings: A Journal of the Christian Spiritual Life* 7, no. 6 (November 1992): 39–40. www.weavings.org.
2. John R. Claypool, *God Is an Amateur* (Cincinnati, Ohio: Forward Movement, 1994), 85–86.
3. Taylor, *An Altar in the World*, 172.
4. Mary Oliver, "The Summer Day," in *New and Selected Poems* (Boston: Beacon Press, 1992).
5. Buechner, *Wishful Thinking*, 119.
6. Parker Palmer, *Let Your Life Speak* (San Francisco: Jossey-Bass, 2000), 16–17.

8. Surprising Wisdom

1. Goodman, "Letting Go," January 1, 2010.
2. Eckhart Tolle, *A New Earth: Awakening to Your Life's Purpose* (London: Penguin Books, 2005), 95–96.
3. Steve Garnaas-Holmes, "Secret Power," *Unfolding Light* (blog), May 27, 2010, http://unfolding-light.blogspot.com.
4. Joan Chittister, "To Live Life More Deeply," December 6, 2010, www.benetvision.org/Ideas_In_Passing/12_06_10.html.
5. Sybil MacBeth, *Praying in Color: Drawing a New Path to God* (Brewster, Mass.: Paraclete Press, 2007).
6. "O Love That Wilt Not Let Me Go," *United Methodist Hymnal* (Nashville, Tenn.: United Methodist Publishing House, 1989), 480.
7. Chittister, "To Live Life More Deeply."

Suggestions for Further Reading

Bankson, Marjory Zoet. *Creative Aging: Rethinking Retirement and Non-Retirement in a Changing World*. Woodstock, Vt.: SkyLight Paths, 2010.

Benson, Robert. *The Echo Within: Finding Your True Calling*. Colorado Springs, Colo.: WaterBrook Press, 2009.

Bieber, Nancy L. *Decision Making & Spiritual Discernment: The Sacred Art of Finding Your Way*. Woodstock, Vt.: SkyLight Paths, 2010.

Bohler, Carolyn Jane. *God the What? What Our Metaphors for God Reveal about Our Beliefs in God*. Woodstock, Vt.: SkyLight Paths, 2008.

Bourgeault, Cynthia. *The Wisdom Way of Knowing: Reclaiming an Ancient Tradition to Awaken the Heart*. San Francisco: Jossey-Bass, 2003.

Chittister, Joan. *The Gift of Years: Growing Older Gracefully*. New York: BlueBridge Books, 2008.

Douty, Linda. *How Can I Let Go If I Don't Know I'm Holding On? Setting Our Souls Free*. Harrisburg, Pa.: Morehouse, 2005.

———. *How Can I See the Light When It's So Dark? Journey to a Thankful Heart*. Harrisburg, Pa.: Morehouse, 2007.

———. *Praying in the Messiness of Life: 7 Ways to Renew Your Relationship with God*. Nashville, Tenn.: Upper Room Books, 2011.

Haas, Jerry P., and R. Jack Hansen. *Shaping a Life of Significance for Retirement*. Nashville, Tenn.: Upper Room Books, 2010.

Hollis, James. *Finding Meaning in the Second Half of Life*. New York: Gotham Books, 2005.

Livingston, Gordon. *Too Soon Old, Too Late Smart: Thirty True Things You Need to Know Now*. New York: Marlowe, 2004.

MacBeth, Sybil. *Praying in Color: Drawing a New Path to God*. Brewster, Mass.: Paraclete Press, 2007.

Markova, Dawna. *I Will Not Die an Unlived Life: Reclaiming Purpose and Passion*. Berkeley, Calif.: Conari Press, 2000.

Nepo, Mark. *The Book of Awakening: Having the Life You Want by Being Present to the Life You Have*. Berkeley, Calif.: Conari Press, 2000.

Norris, Gunilla. *Being Home: Discovering the Spiritual in the Everyday.* Mahwah, N.J.: HiddenSpring, 2001.

Palmer, Parker. *Let Your Life Speak: Listening for the Voice of Vocation.* San Francisco: Jossey-Bass, 2000.

Richards, Marty. *Caresharing: A Reciprocal Approach to Caregiving and Care Receiving in the Complexities of Aging, Illness or Disability.* Woodstock, Vt.: SkyLight Paths, 2009.

Ryan, Thomas. *Soul Fire: Accessing Your Creativity.* Woodstock, Vt.: SkyLight Paths, 2008.

Simpson, Robert, and Anne Simpson. *Through the Wilderness of Alzheimer's: A Guide in Two Voices.* Minneapolis, Minn.: Augsburg Fortress, 1999.

Snyder, Lisa. *Living Your Best with Early-Stage Alzheimer's: An Essential Guide.* North Branch, Minn: Sunrise River Press, 2010.

Srode, Molly. *Creating a Spiritual Retirement: A Guide to the Unseen Possibilities in Our Lives.* Woodstock, Vt.: SkyLight Paths, 2003.

Srode, Molly, and Bernie Srode. *Keeping Spiritual Balance As We Grow Older: More Than 65 Creative Ways to Use Purpose, Prayer, and the Power of Spirit to Build a Meaningful Retirement.* Woodstock, Vt.: SkyLight Paths, 2004.

Taylor, Barbara Brown. *An Altar in the World: A Geography of Faith.* New York: HarperOne, 2009.

Taylor, Richard. *Alzheimer's from the Inside Out.* Baltimore: Health Professions Press, 2007.

Thompson, Marjorie J. *Soul Feast: An Invitation to the Christian Spiritual Life.* Louisville, Ky.: Westminster John Knox Press, 2005.

Tolle, Eckhart. *A New Earth: Awakening to Your Life's Purpose.* New York: Plume, 2005.

Ulanov, Ann, and Barry Ulanov. *Primary Speech: A Psychology of Prayer.* Atlanta: Westminster John Knox Press, 1982.

Vennard, Jane E. *Praying with Body and Soul: A Way to Intimacy with God.* Minneapolis, Minn.: Augsburg Fortress, 1998.

Spiritual Poetry—The Mystic Poets

Experience these mystic poets as you never have before. Each beautiful, compact book includes a brief introduction to the poet's time and place, a summary of the major themes of the poet's mysticism and religious tradition, essential selections from the poet's most important works, and an appreciative preface by a contemporary spiritual writer.

Hafiz
The Mystic Poets
Translated and with Notes by Gertrude Bell
Preface by Ibrahim Gamard
Hafiz is known throughout the world as Persia's greatest poet, with sales of his poems in Iran today only surpassed by those of the Qur'an itself. His probing and joyful verse speaks to people from all backgrounds who long to taste and feel divine love and experience harmony with all living things.
5 x 7¼, 144 pp, HC, 978-1-59473-009-2 **$16.99**

Hopkins
The Mystic Poets
Preface by Rev. Thomas Ryan, CSP
Gerard Manley Hopkins, Christian mystical poet, is beloved for his use of fresh language and startling metaphors to describe the world around him. Although his verse is lovely, beneath the surface lies a searching soul, wrestling with and yearning for God.
5 x 7¼, 112 pp, HC, 978-1-59473-010-8 **$16.99**

Tagore
The Mystic Poets
Preface by Swami Adiswarananda
Rabindranath Tagore is often considered the Shakespeare of modern India. A great mystic, Tagore was the teacher of W. B. Yeats and Robert Frost, the close friend of Albert Einstein and Mahatma Gandhi, and the winner of the Nobel Prize for Literature. This beautiful sampling of Tagore's two most important works, *The Gardener* and *Gitanjali*, offers a glimpse into his spiritual vision that has inspired people around the world.
5 x 7¼, 144 pp, HC, 978-1-59473-008-5 **$16.99**

Whitman
The Mystic Poets
Preface by Gary David Comstock
Walt Whitman was the most innovative and influential poet of the nineteenth century. This beautiful sampling of Whitman's most important poetry from *Leaves of Grass*, and selections from his prose writings, offers a glimpse into the spiritual side of his most radical themes—love for country, love for others and love of self.
5 x 7¼, 192 pp, HC, 978-1-59473-041-2 **$16.99**

Or phone, fax, mail or e-mail to: SKYLIGHT PATHS Publishing
Sunset Farm Offices, Route 4 • P.O. Box 237 • Woodstock, Vermont 05091
Tel: (802) 457-4000 • Fax: (802) 457-4004 • www.skylightpaths.com
Credit card orders: (800) 962-4544 (8:30AM–5:30PM ET Monday–Friday)
Generous discounts on quantity orders. SATISFACTION GUARANTEED. Prices subject to change.

Spirituality of the Seasons

Autumn: A Spiritual Biography of the Season
Edited by Gary Schmidt and Susan M. Felch; Illus. by Mary Azarian
Rejoice in autumn as a time of preparation and reflection. Includes Wendell Berry, David James Duncan, Robert Frost, A. Bartlett Giamatti, E. B. White, P. D. James, Julian of Norwich, Garret Keizer, Tracy Kidder, Anne Lamott, May Sarton.
6 x 9, 320 pp, b/w illus., Quality PB, 978-1-59473-118-1 **$18.99**

Spring: A Spiritual Biography of the Season
Edited by Gary Schmidt and Susan M. Felch; Illus. by Mary Azarian
Explore the gentle unfurling of spring and reflect on how nature celebrates rebirth and renewal. Includes Jane Kenyon, Lucy Larcom, Harry Thurston, Nathaniel Hawthorne, Noel Perrin, Annie Dillard, Martha Ballard, Barbara Kingsolver, Dorothy Wordsworth, Donald Hall, David Brill, Lionel Basney, Isak Dinesen, Paul Laurence Dunbar. 6 x 9, 352 pp, b/w illus., Quality PB, 978-1-59473-246-1 **$18.99**

Summer: A Spiritual Biography of the Season
Edited by Gary Schmidt and Susan M. Felch; Illus. by Barry Moser
"A sumptuous banquet.... These selections lift up an exquisite wholeness found within an everyday sophistication." — ★ *Publishers Weekly* starred review
Includes Anne Lamott, Luci Shaw, Ray Bradbury, Richard Selzer, Thomas Lynch, Walt Whitman, Carl Sandburg, Sherman Alexie, Madeleine L'Engle, Jamaica Kincaid.
6 x 9, 304 pp, b/w illus., Quality PB, 978-1-59473-183-9 **$18.99**
HC, 978-1-59473-083-2 **$21.99**

Winter: A Spiritual Biography of the Season
Edited by Gary Schmidt and Susan M. Felch; Illus. by Barry Moser
"This outstanding anthology features top-flight nature and spirituality writers on the fierce, inexorable season of winter.... Remarkably lively and warm, despite the icy subject." — ★ *Publishers Weekly* starred review
Includes Will Campbell, Rachel Carson, Annie Dillard, Donald Hall, Ron Hansen, Jane Kenyon, Jamaica Kincaid, Barry Lopez, Kathleen Norris, John Updike, E. B. White.
6 x 9, 288 pp, b/w illus., Deluxe PB w/ flaps, 978-1-893361-92-8 **$18.95**
HC, 978-1-893361-53-9 **$21.95**

Spirituality / Animal Companions

Blessing the Animals: Prayers and Ceremonies to Celebrate God's Creatures, Wild and Tame *Edited and with Introductions by Lynn L. Caruso*
5¼ x 7¼, 256 pp, Quality PB, 978-1-59473-253-9 **$15.99**; HC, 978-1-59473-145-7 **$19.99**

Remembering My Pet: A Kid's Own Spiritual Workbook for When a Pet Dies
by Nechama Liss-Levinson, PhD, and Rev. Molly Phinney Baskette, MDiv; Foreword by Lynn L. Caruso
8 x 10, 48 pp, 2-color text, HC, 978-1-59473-221-8 **$16.99**

What Animals Can Teach Us about Spirituality: Inspiring Lessons from Wild and Tame Creatures *by Diana L. Guerrero* 6 x 9, 176 pp, Quality PB, 978-1-893361-84-3 **$16.95**

Spirituality—A Week Inside

Lighting the Lamp of Wisdom: A Week Inside a Yoga Ashram
by John Ittner; Foreword by Dr. David Frawley
6 x 9, 192 pp, b/w photos, Quality PB, 978-1-893361-52-2 **$15.95**

Making a Heart for God: A Week Inside a Catholic Monastery
by Dianne Aprile; Foreword by Brother Patrick Hart, OCSO
6 x 9, 224 pp, b/w photos, Quality PB, 978-1-893361-49-2 **$16.95**

Waking Up: A Week Inside a Zen Monastery
by Jack Maguire; Foreword by John Daido Loori, Roshi
6 x 9, 224 pp, b/w photos, Quality PB, 978-1-893361-55-3 **$16.95**; HC, 978-1-893361-13-3 **$21.95**

Spirituality

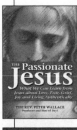

The Passionate Jesus: What We Can Learn from Jesus about Love, Fear, Grief, Joy and Living Authentically
By The Rev. Peter Wallace
Reveals Jesus as a passionate figure who was involved, present, connected, honest and direct with others and encourages you to build personal authenticity in every area of your own life.
6 x 9, 208 pp, Quality PB, 978-1-59473-393-2 **$18.99**

Gathering at God's Table: The Meaning of Mission in the Feast of Faith
By Katharine Jefferts Schori
A profound reminder of our role in the larger frame of God's dream for a restored and reconciled world. 6 x 9, 256 pp, HC, 978-1-59473-316-1 **$21.99**

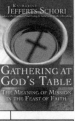

The Heartbeat of God: Finding the Sacred in the Middle of Everything
By Katharine Jefferts Schori; Foreword by Joan Chittister, OSB
Explores our connections to other people, to other nations and with the environment through the lens of faith. 6 x 9, 240 pp, HC, 978-1-59473-292-8 **$21.99**

A Dangerous Dozen: Twelve Christians Who Threatened the Status Quo but Taught Us to Live Like Jesus
By the Rev. Canon C. K. Robertson, PhD; Foreword by Archbishop Desmond Tutu
Profiles twelve visionary men and women who challenged society and showed the world a different way of living. 6 x 9, 208 pp, Quality PB, 978-1-59473-298-0 **$16.99**

Decision Making & Spiritual Discernment: The Sacred Art of Finding Your Way *By Nancy L Bieber*
Presents three essential aspects of Spirit-led decision making: willingness, attentiveness and responsiveness. 5½ x 8½, 208 pp, Quality PB, 978-1-59473-289-8 **$16.99**

Laugh Your Way to Grace: Reclaiming the Spiritual Power of Humor
By Rev. Susan Sparks A powerful, humorous case for laughter as a spiritual, healing path. 6 x 9, 176 pp, Quality PB, 978-1-59473-280-5 **$16.99**

Bread, Body, Spirit: Finding the Sacred in Food
Edited and with Introductions by Alice Peck 6 x 9, 224 pp, Quality PB, 978-1-59473-242-3 **$19.99**

Claiming Earth as Common Ground: The Ecological Crisis through the Lens of Faith
By Andrea Cohen-Kiener; Foreword by Rev. Sally Bingham
6 x 9, 192 pp, Quality PB, 978-1-59473-261-4 **$16.99**

Creating a Spiritual Retirement: A Guide to the Unseen Possibilities in Our Lives
By Molly Srode 6 x 9, 208 pp, b/w photos, Quality PB, 978-1-59473-050-4 **$14.99**

Creative Aging: Rethinking Retirement and Non-Retirement in a Changing World
By Marjory Zoet Bankson 6 x 9, 160 pp, Quality PB, 978-1-59473-281-2 **$16.99**

Keeping Spiritual Balance as We Grow Older: More than 65 Creative Ways to Use Purpose, Prayer, and the Power of Spirit to Build a Meaningful Retirement
By Molly and Bernie Srode 8 x 8, 224 pp, Quality PB, 978-1-59473-042-9 **$16.99**

Hearing the Call across Traditions: Readings on Faith and Service
Edited by Adam Davis; Foreword by Eboo Patel 6 x 9, 352 pp, Quality PB, 978-1-59473-303-1 **$18.99**

Honoring Motherhood: Prayers, Ceremonies & Blessings
Edited and with Introductions by Lynn L Caruso
5 x 7¼, 272 pp, Quality PB, 978-1-58473-384-0 **$9.99**; HC, 978-1-59473-239-3 **$19.99**

The Losses of Our Lives: The Sacred Gifts of Renewal in Everyday Loss
By Dr. Nancy Copeland-Payton 6 x 9, 192 pp, HC, 978-1-59473-271-3 **$19.99**

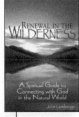

Renewal in the Wilderness: A Spiritual Guide to Connecting with God in the Natural World *By John Lionberger* 6 x 9, 176 pp, b/w photos, Quality PB, 978-1-59473-219-5 **$16.99**

Soul Fire: Accessing Your Creativity
By Thomas Ryan, CSP 6 x 9, 160 pp, Quality PB, 978-1-59473-243-0 **$16.99**

A Spirituality for Brokenness: Discovering Your Deepest Self in Difficult Times
By Terry Taylor 6 x 9, 176 pp, Quality PB, 978-1-59473-229-4 **$16.99**

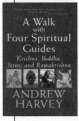

A Walk with Four Spiritual Guides: Krishna, Buddha, Jesus, and Ramakrishna
By Andrew Harvey 5½ x 8½, 192 pp, b/w photos & illus., Quality PB, 978-1-59473-138-9 **$15.99**

Spirituality & Crafts

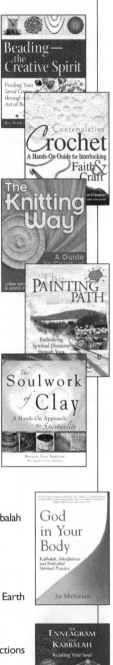

Beading—The Creative Spirit: Finding Your Sacred Center through the Art of Beadwork *by Rev. Wendy Ellsworth*
Invites you on a spiritual pilgrimage into the kaleidoscope world of glass and color. 7 x 9, 240 pp, 8-page color insert, 40+ b/w photos and 40 diagrams, Quality PB, 978-1-59473-267-6 **$18.99**

Contemplative Crochet: A Hands-On Guide for Interlocking Faith and Craft *by Cindy Crandall-Frazier; Foreword by Linda Skolnik*
Illuminates the spiritual lessons you can learn through crocheting.
7 x 9, 208 pp, b/w photos, Quality PB, 978-1-59473-238-6 **$16.99**

The Knitting Way: A Guide to Spiritual Self-Discovery
by Linda Skolnik and Janice MacDaniels Examines how you can explore and strengthen your spiritual life through knitting.
7 x 9, 240 pp, b/w photos, Quality PB, 978-1-59473-079-5 **$16.99**

The Painting Path: Embodying Spiritual Discovery through Yoga, Brush and Color *by Linda Novick; Foreword by Richard Segalman*
Explores the divine connection you can experience through art.
7 x 9, 208 pp, 8-page color insert, plus b/w photos, Quality PB, 978-1-59473-226-3 **$18.99**

The Quilting Path: A Guide to Spiritual Discovery through Fabric, Thread and Kabbalah *by Louise Silk*
Explores how to cultivate personal growth through quilt making.
7 x 9, 192 pp, b/w photos and illus., Quality PB, 978-1-59473-206-5 **$16.99**

The Scrapbooking Journey: A Hands-On Guide to Spiritual Discovery
by Cory Richardson-Lauve; Foreword by Stacy Julian Reveals how this craft can become a practice used to deepen and shape your life.
7 x 9, 176 pp, 8-page color insert, plus b/w photos, Quality PB, 978-1-59473-216-4 **$18.99**

The Soulwork of Clay: A Hands-On Approach to Spirituality
by Marjory Zoet Bankson; Photos by Peter Bankson
Takes you through the seven-step process of making clay into a pot, drawing parallels at each stage to the process of spiritual growth.
7 x 9, 192 pp, b/w photos, Quality PB, 978-1-59473-249-2 **$16.99**

Kabbalah / Enneagram
(Books from Jewish Lights Publishing, SkyLight Paths' sister imprint)

Cast in God's Image: Discover Your Personality Type Using the Enneagram and Kabbalah
by Rabbi Howard A. Addison, PhD 7 x 9, 176 pp, Quality PB, 978-1-58023-124-4 **$16.95**

Ehyeh: A Kabbalah for Tomorrow *by Rabbi Arthur Green, PhD*
6 x 9, 224 pp, Quality PB, 978-1-58023-213-5 **$18.99**

The Enneagram and Kabbalah, 2nd Edition: Reading Your Soul
by Rabbi Howard A. Addison, PhD 6 x 9, 192 pp, Quality PB, 978-1-58023-229-6 **$16.99**

The Gift of Kabbalah: Discovering the Secrets of Heaven, Renewing Your Life on Earth
by Tamar Frankiel, PhD 6 x 9, 256 pp, Quality PB, 978-1-58023-141-1 **$16.95**

God in Your Body: Kabbalah, Mindfulness and Embodied Spiritual Practice
by Jay Michaelson 6 x 9, 272 pp, Quality PB, 978-1-58023-304-0 **$18.99**

Jewish Mysticism and the Spiritual Life: Classical Texts, Contemporary Reflections
Edited by Dr. Lawrence Fine, Dr. Eitan Fishbane and Rabbi Or N. Rose
6 x 9, 256 pp, HC, 978-1-58023-434-4 **$24.99**

Kabbalah: A Brief Introduction for Christians
by Tamar Frankiel, PhD 5½ x 8½, 208 pp, Quality PB, 978-1-58023-303-3 **$16.99**

Zohar: Annotated & Explained *Translation & Annotation by Daniel C. Matt;*
Foreword by Andrew Harvey 5½ x 8½, 176 pp, Quality PB, 978-1-893361-51-5 **$15.99**

Spiritual Practice

Fly Fishing—The Sacred Art: Casting a Fly as a Spiritual Practice
by Rabbi Eric Eisenkramer and Rev. Michael Attas, MD
Illuminates what fly fishing can teach you about reflection, awe and wonder; the benefits of solitude; the blessing of community and the search for the Divine.
5½ x 8½, 192 pp (est), Quality PB, 978-1-59473-299-7 **$16.99**

Lectio Divina—The Sacred Art: Transforming Words & Images into Heart-Centered Prayer *by Christine Valters Paintner, PhD*
Expands the practice of sacred reading beyond scriptural texts and makes it accessible in contemporary life. 5½ x 8½, 192 pp (est), Quality PB, 978-1-59473-300-0 **$16.99**

Haiku—The Sacred Art: A Spiritual Practice in Three Lines
by Margaret D. McGee 5½ x 8½, 192 pp, Quality PB, 978-1-59473-269-0 **$16.99**

Dance—The Sacred Art: The Joy of Movement as a Spiritual Practice
by Cynthia Winton-Henry 5½ x 8½, 224 pp, Quality PB, 978-1-59473-268-3 **$16.99**

Spiritual Adventures in the Snow: Skiing & Snowboarding as Renewal for Your Soul *by Dr. Marcia McFee and Rev. Karen Foster; Foreword by Paul Arthur*
5½ x 8½, 208 pp, Quality PB, 978-1-59473-270-6 **$16.99**

Divining the Body: Reclaim the Holiness of Your Physical Self *by Jan Phillips*
8 x 8, 256 pp, Quality PB, 978-1-59473-080-1 **$16.99**

Everyday Herbs in Spiritual Life: A Guide to Many Practices
by Michael J. Caduto; Foreword by Rosemary Gladstar
7 x 9, 208 pp, 20+ b/w illus., Quality PB, 978-1-59473-174-7 **$16.99**

Giving—The Sacred Art: Creating a Lifestyle of Generosity
by Lauren Tyler Wright 5½ x 8½, 208 pp, Quality PB, 978-1-59473-224-9 **$16.99**

Hospitality—The Sacred Art: Discovering the Hidden Spiritual Power of Invitation and Welcome *by Rev. Nanette Sawyer; Foreword by Rev. Dirk Ficca*
5½ x 8½, 208 pp, Quality PB, 978-1-59473-228-7 **$16.99**

Labyrinths from the Outside In: Walking to Spiritual Insight—A Beginner's Guide
by Donna Schaper and Carole Ann Camp
6 x 9, 208 pp, b/w illus. and photos, Quality PB, 978-1-893361-18-8 **$16.95**

Practicing the Sacred Art of Listening: A Guide to Enrich Your Relationships and Kindle Your Spiritual Life *by Kay Lindahl* 8 x 8, 176 pp, Quality PB, 978-1-893361-85-0 **$16.95**

Recovery—The Sacred Art: The Twelve Steps as Spiritual Practice *by Rami Shapiro; Foreword by Joan Borysenko, PhD* 5½ x 8½, 240 pp, Quality PB, 978-1-59473-259-1 **$16.99**

Running—The Sacred Art: Preparing to Practice *by Dr. Warren A. Kay; Foreword by Kristin Armstrong* 5½ x 8½, 160 pp, Quality PB, 978-1-59473-227-0 **$16.99**

The Sacred Art of Chant: Preparing to Practice
by Ana Hernández 5½ x 8½, 192 pp, Quality PB, 978-1-59473-036-8 **$15.99**

The Sacred Art of Fasting: Preparing to Practice
by Thomas Ryan, CSP 5½ x 8½, 192 pp, Quality PB, 978-1-59473-078-8 **$15.99**

The Sacred Art of Forgiveness: Forgiving Ourselves and Others through God's Grace
by Marcia Ford 8 x 8, 176 pp, Quality PB, 978-1-59473-175-4 **$18.99**

The Sacred Art of Listening: Forty Reflections for Cultivating a Spiritual Practice
by Kay Lindahl; Illus. by Amy Schnapper 8 x 8, 160 pp, b/w illus., Quality PB, 978-1-893361-44-7 **$16.99**

The Sacred Art of Lovingkindness: Preparing to Practice
by Rabbi Rami Shapiro; Foreword by Marcia Ford 5½ x 8½, 176 pp, Quality PB, 978-1-59473-151-8 **$16.99**

Sacred Attention: A Spiritual Practice for Finding God in the Moment
by Margaret D. McGee 6 x 9, 144 pp, Quality PB, 978-1-59473-291-1 **$16.99**

Soul Fire: Accessing Your Creativity
by Thomas Ryan, CSP 6 x 9, 160 pp, Quality PB, 978-1-59473-243-0 **$16.99**

Thanking & Blessing—The Sacred Art: Spiritual Vitality through Gratefulness
by Jay Marshall, PhD; Foreword by Philip Gulley 5½ x 8½, 176 pp, Quality PB, 978-1-59473-231-7 **$16.99**

Prayer / Meditation

Men Pray: Voices of Strength, Faith, Healing, Hope and Courage
Created by the Editors at SkyLight Paths
Celebrates the rich variety of ways men around the world have called out to the Divine—with words of joy, praise, gratitude, wonder, petition and even anger—from the ancient world up to our own day.
5 x 7¼, 192 pp, HC, 978-1-59473-395-6 **$16.99**

Honest to God Prayer: Spirituality as Awareness, Empowerment, Relinquishment and Paradox
By Kent Ira Groff
For those turned off by shopworn religious language, offers innovative ways to pray based on both Native American traditions and Ignatian spirituality.
6 x 9, 192 pp, Quality PB, 978-1-59473-433-5 **$16.99**

Sacred Attention: A Spiritual Practice for Finding God in the Moment
By Margaret D. McGee
Framed on the Christian liturgical year, this inspiring guide explores ways to develop a practice of attention as a means of talking—and listening—to God.
6 x 9, 144 pp, Quality PB, 978-1-59473-291-1 **$16.99**

Women of Color Pray: Voices of Strength, Faith, Healing, Hope and Courage
Edited and with Introductions by Christal M. Jackson
Through these prayers, poetry, lyrics, meditations and affirmations, you will share in the strong and undeniable connection women of color share with God.
5 x 7¼, 208 pp, Quality PB, 978-1-59473-077-1 **$15.99**

Living into Hope: A Call to Spiritual Action for Such a Time as This
By Rev. Dr. Joan Brown Campbell; Foreword by Karen Armstrong
6 x 9, 208 pp, HC, 978-1-59473-283-6 **$21.99**

Praying with Our Hands: 21 Practices of Embodied Prayer from the World's Spiritual Traditions *By Jon M. Sweeney; Photos by Jennifer J. Wilson; Foreword by Mother Tessa Bielecki; Afterword by Taitetsu Unno, PhD*
8 x 8, 96 pp, 22 duotone photos, Quality PB, 978-1-893361-16-4 **$16.95**

Secrets of Prayer: A Multifaith Guide to Creating Personal Prayer in Your Life
By Nancy Corcoran, CSJ
6 x 9, 160 pp, Quality PB, 978-1-59473-215-7 **$16.99**

Three Gates to Meditation Practice: A Personal Journey into Sufism, Buddhism, and Judaism *By David A. Cooper* 5½ x 8½, 240 pp, Quality PB, 978-1-893361-22-5 **$16.95**

Prayer / M. Basil Pennington, OCSO

Finding Grace at the Center, 3rd Edition: The Beginning of Centering Prayer *With Thomas Keating, OCSO, and Thomas E. Clarke, SJ; Foreword by Rev. Cynthia Bourgeault, PhD* A practical guide to a simple and beautiful form of meditative prayer. 5 x 7¼,128 pp, Quality PB, 978-1-59473-182-2 **$12.99**

The Monks of Mount Athos: A Western Monk's Extraordinary Spiritual Journey on Eastern Holy Ground *Foreword by Archimandrite Dionysios*
Explores the landscape, monastic communities and food of Athos.
6 x 9, 352 pp, Quality PB, 978-1-893361-78-2 **$18.95**

Psalms: A Spiritual Commentary *Illus. by Phillip Ratner*
Reflections on some of the most beloved passages from the Bible's most widely read book. 6 x 9, 176 pp, 24 full-page b/w illus., Quality PB, 978-1-59473-234-8 **$16.99**

The Song of Songs: A Spiritual Commentary *Illus. by Phillip Ratner*
Explore the Bible's most challenging mystical text.
6 x 9, 160 pp, 14 full-page b/w illus., Quality PB, 978-1-59473-235-5 **$16.99**
HC, 978-1-59473-004-7 **$19.99**

Bible Stories / Folktales

Abraham's Bind & Other Bible Tales of Trickery, Folly, Mercy and Love by Michael J. Caduto
New retellings of episodes in the lives of familiar biblical characters explore relevant life lessons.   6 x 9, 224 pp, HC, 978-1-59473-186-0 **$19.99**

Daughters of the Desert: Stories of Remarkable Women from Christian, Jewish and Muslim Traditions by Claire Rudolf Murphy,
Meghan Nuttall Sayres, Mary Cronk Farrell, Sarah Conover and Betsy Wharton
Breathes new life into the old tales of our female ancestors in faith. Uses traditional scriptural passages as starting points, then with vivid detail fills in historical context and place. Chapters reveal the voices of Sarah, Hagar, Huldah, Esther, Salome, Mary Magdalene, Lydia, Khadija, Fatima and many more. Historical fiction ideal for readers of all ages.
5½ x 8½, 192 pp, Quality PB, 978-1-59473-106-8 **$14.99**   Inc. reader's discussion guide
HC, 978-1-893361-72-0 **$19.95**

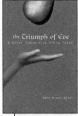

The Triumph of Eve & Other Subversive Bible Tales
by Matt Biers-Ariel
These engaging retellings of familiar Bible stories are witty, often hilarious and always profound. They invite you to grapple with questions and issues that are often hidden in the original texts.
5½ x 8½, 192 pp, Quality PB, 978-1-59473-176-1 **$14.99**

Also available: **The Triumph of Eve Teacher's Guide**
8½ x 11, 44 pp, PB, 978-1-59473-152-5 **$8.99**

Wisdom in the Telling
Finding Inspiration and Grace in Traditional Folktales and Myths Retold
by Lorraine Hartin-Gelardi
6 x 9, 192 pp, HC, 978-1-59473-185-3 **$19.99**

Religious Etiquette / Reference

How to Be a Perfect Stranger, 5th Edition: The Essential Religious Etiquette Handbook *Edited by Stuart M. Matlins and Arthur J. Magida*
The indispensable guidebook to help the well-meaning guest when visiting other people's religious ceremonies. A straightforward guide to the rituals and celebrations of the major religions and denominations in the United States and Canada from the perspective of an interested guest of any other faith, based on information obtained from authorities of each religion. Belongs in every living room, library and office. Covers:

African American Methodist Churches • Assemblies of God • Bahá'í Faith • Baptist • Buddhist • Christian Church (Disciples of Christ) • Christian Science (Church of Christ, Scientist) • Churches of Christ • Episcopalian and Anglican • Hindu • Islam • Jehovah's Witnesses • Jewish • Lutheran • Mennonite/Amish • Methodist • Mormon (Church of Jesus Christ of Latter-day Saints) • Native American/First Nations • Orthodox Churches • Pentecostal Church of God • Presbyterian • Quaker (Religious Society of Friends) • Reformed Church in America/Canada • Roman Catholic • Seventh-day Adventist • Sikh • Unitarian Universalist • United Church of Canada • United Church of Christ

"The things Miss Manners forgot to tell us about religion."
—*Los Angeles Times*

"Finally, for those inclined to undertake their own spiritual journeys ... tells visitors what to expect."   —*New York Times*

6 x 9, 432 pp, Quality PB, 978-1-59473-294-2 **$19.99**

The Perfect Stranger's Guide to Funerals and Grieving Practices: A Guide to Etiquette in Other People's Religious Ceremonies *Edited by Stuart M. Matlins*
6 x 9, 240 pp, Quality PB, 978-1-893361-20-1 **$16.95**

The Perfect Stranger's Guide to Wedding Ceremonies: A Guide to Etiquette in Other People's Religious Ceremonies *Edited by Stuart M. Matlins*
6 x 9, 208 pp, Quality PB, 978-1-893361-19-5 **$16.95**

Judaism / Christianity / Islam / Interfaith

Spiritual Gems of Islam: Insights & Practices from the Qur'an, Hadith, Rumi & Muslim Teaching Stories to Enlighten the Heart & Mind
By Imam Jamal Rahman
Invites you—no matter what your practice may be—to access the treasure chest of Islamic spirituality and use its wealth in your own journey.
6 x 9, 256 pp, Quality PB, 978-1-59473-430-4 **$16.99**

All Politics Is Religious: Speaking Faith to the Media, Policy Makers and Community   *By Rabbi Dennis S. Ross; Foreword by Rev. Barry W. Lynn*
Provides ideas and strategies for expressing a clear, forceful and progressive religious point of view that is all too often overlooked and under-represented in public discourse.   6 x 9, 192 pp, Quality PB, 978-1-59473-374-1 **$18.99**

Religion Gone Astray: What We Found at the Heart of Interfaith
By Pastor Don Mackenzie, Rabbi Ted Falcon and Imam Jamal Rahman
Welcome to the deeper dimensions of interfaith dialogue—exploring that which divides us personally, spiritually and institutionally.
6 x 9, 192 pp, Quality PB, 978-1-59473-317-8 **$16.99**

Getting to the Heart of Interfaith: The Eye-Opening, Hope-Filled Friendship of a Pastor, a Rabbi & an Imam   *By Pastor Don Mackenzie, Rabbi Ted Falcon and Imam Jamal Rahman*
6 x 9, 192 pp, Quality PB, 978-1-59473-263-8 **$16.99**

Hearing the Call across Traditions: Readings on Faith and Service
Edited by Adam Davis; Foreword by Eboo Patel
6 x 9, 352 pp, Quality PB, 978-1-59473-303-1 **$18.99**

How to Do Good & Avoid Evil: A Global Ethic from the Sources of Judaism
By Hans Küng and Rabbi Walter Homolka; Translated by Rev. Dr. John Bowden
6 x 9, 224 pp, HC, 978-1-59473-255-3 **$19.99**

Blessed Relief: What Christians Can Learn from Buddhists about Suffering
By Gordon Peerman   6 x 9, 208 pp, Quality PB, 978-1-59473-252-2 **$16.99**

Christians & Jews—Faith to Faith: Tragic History, Promising Present, Fragile Future   *By Rabbi James Rudin*   6 x 9, 288 pp, HC, 978-1-58023-432-0 **$24.99***

Christians & Jews in Dialogue: Learning in the Presence of the Other   *By Mary C. Boys and Sara S. Lee; Foreword by Dorothy C. Bass*   6 x 9, 240 pp, Quality PB, 978-1-59473-254-6 **$18.99**

InterActive Faith: The Essential Interreligious Community-Building Handbook
Edited by Rev. Bud Heckman with Rori Picker Neiss; Foreword by Rev. Dirk Ficca
6 x 9, 304 pp, Quality PB, 978-1-59473-273-7 **$16.99**; HC, 978-1-59473-237-9 **$29.99**

The Jewish Approach to God: A Brief Introduction for Christians
By Rabbi Neil Gillman, PhD 5½ x 8½, 192 pp, Quality PB, 978-1-58023-190-9 **$16.95***

The Jewish Approach to Repairing the World (*Tikkun Olam*): A Brief Introduction for Christians   *By Rabbi Elliot N. Dorff, PhD, with Rev. Cory Willson*
5½ x 8½, 256 pp, Quality PB, 978-1-58023-349-1 **$16.99***

The Jewish Connection to Israel, the Promised Land: A Brief Introduction for Christians   *By Rabbi Eugene Korn, PhD* 5½ x 8½, 192 pp, Quality PB, 978-1-58023-318-7 **$14.99***

Jewish Holidays: A Brief Introduction for Christians   *By Rabbi Kerry M. Olitzky and Rabbi Daniel Judson* 5½ x 8½, 176 pp, Quality PB, 978-1-58023-302-6 **$16.99***

Jewish Ritual: A Brief Introduction for Christians
By Rabbi Kerry M. Olitzky and Rabbi Daniel Judson 5½ x 8½, 144 pp, Quality PB, 978-1-58023-210-4 **$14.99***

Jewish Spirituality: A Brief Introduction for Christians   *By Rabbi Lawrence Kushner*
5½ x 8½, 112 pp, Quality PB, 978-1-58023-150-3 **$12.95***

* A book from Jewish Lights, SkyLight Paths' sister imprint

Children's Spirituality

ENDORSED BY CATHOLIC, PROTESTANT, JEWISH, AND BUDDHIST RELIGIOUS LEADERS

Adam & Eve's First Sunset: God's New Day
by Sandy Eisenberg Sasso; Full-color illus. by Joani Keller Rothenberg 9 x 12, 32 pp, Full-color illus., HC, 978-1-58023-177-0 **$17.95*** *For ages 4 & up*

Because Nothing Looks Like God
by Lawrence Kushner and Karen Kushner; Full-color illus. by Dawn W. Majewski
Invites parents and children to explore the questions we all have about God.
11 x 8½, 32 pp, Full-color illus., HC, 978-1-58023-092-6 **$17.99*** *For ages 4 & up*
Also available: **Teacher's Guide** 8½ x 11, 22 pp, PB, 978-1-58023-140-4 **$6.95**

But God Remembered: Stories of Women from Creation to the Promised Land
by Sandy Eisenberg Sasso; Full-color illus. by Bethanne Andersen
A fascinating collection of four different stories of women only briefly mentioned in biblical tradition and religious texts.
9 x 12, 32 pp, Full-color illus., Quality PB, 978-1-58023-372-9 **$8.99*** *For ages 8 & up*

Cain & Abel: Finding the Fruits of Peace
by Sandy Eisenberg Sasso; Full-color illus. by Joani Keller Rothenberg
A sensitive recasting of the ancient tale shows we have the power to deal with anger in positive ways. "Editor's Choice." —American Library Association's *Booklist*
9 x 12, 32 pp, Full-color illus., HC, 978-1-58023-123-7 **$16.95*** *For ages 5 & up*

Does God Hear My Prayer?
by August Gold; Full-color photos by Diane Hardy Waller
Introduces preschoolers and young readers to prayer and how it helps them express their own emotions.
10 x 8½, 32 pp, Full-color photo illus., Quality PB, 978-1-59473-102-0 **$8.99** *For ages 3–6*

The 11th Commandment: Wisdom from Our Children *by The Children of America*
"If there were an Eleventh Commandment, what would it be?" Children of many religious denominations across America answer this question—in their own drawings and words. "A rare book of spiritual celebration for all people, of all ages, for all time." —*Bookviews* 8 x 10, 48 pp, Full-color illus., HC, 978-1-879045-46-0 **$16.95***
For all ages

For Heaven's Sake *by Sandy Eisenberg Sasso; Full-color illus. by Kathryn Kunz Finney*
Heaven is often found where you least expect it.
9 x 12, 32 pp, Full-color illus., HC, 978-1-58023-054-4 **$16.95*** *For ages 4 & up*

God in Between *by Sandy Eisenberg Sasso; Full-color illus. by Sally Sweetland*
A magical, mythical tale that teaches that God can be found where we are.
9 x 12, 32 pp, Full-color illus., HC, 978-1-879045-86-6 **$16.95*** *For ages 4 & up*

God's Paintbrush: Special 10th Anniversary Edition
by Sandy Eisenberg Sasso; Full-color illus. by Annette Compton
Invites children of all faiths and backgrounds to encounter God through moments in their own lives. 11 x 8½, 32 pp, Full-color illus., HC, 978-1-58023-195-4 **$17.95*** *For ages 4 & up*
Also available: **God's Paintbrush Teacher's Guide**
8½ x 11, 32 pp, PB, 978-1-879045-57-6 **$8.95**

God's Paintbrush Celebration Kit: A Spiritual Activity Kit for Teachers and Students of All Faiths, All Backgrounds 9½ x 12, 40 Full-color Activity Sheets & Teacher Folder
w/ complete instructions, HC, 978-1-58023-050-6 **$21.95**
Additional activity sheets available:
8-Student Activity Sheet Pack (40 sheets/5 sessions), 978-1-58023-058-2 **$19.95**
Single-Student Activity Sheet Pack (5 sessions), 978-1-58023-059-9 **$3.95**

I Am God's Paintbrush (A Board Book)
by Sandy Eisenberg Sasso; Full-color illus. by Annette Compton
5 x 5, 24 pp, Full-color illus., Board Book, 978-1-59473-265-2 **$7.99** *For ages 0–4*

* A book from Jewish Lights, SkyLight Paths' sister imprint

Children's Spirituality

Remembering My Grandparent: A Kid's Own Grief Workbook in the Christian Tradition *by Nechama Liss-Levinson, PhD, and Rev. Molly Phinney Baskette, MDiv* 8 x 10, 48 pp, 2-color text, HC, 978-1-59473-212-6 **$16.99** *For ages 7 & up*

Does God Ever Sleep? *by Joan Sauro, CSJ*
A charming nighttime reminder that God is always present in our lives.
10 x 8½, 32 pp, Full-color photos, Quality PB, 978-1-59473-110-5 **$8.99** *For ages 3–6*

Does God Forgive Me? *by August Gold; Full-color photos by Diane Hardy Waller*
Gently shows how God forgives all that we do if we are truly sorry.
10 x 8½, 32 pp, Full-color photos, Quality PB, 978-1-59473-142-6 **$8.99** *For ages 3–6*

God Said Amen *by Sandy Eisenberg Sasso; Full-color illus. by Avi Katz*
A warm and inspiring tale that shows us that we need only reach out to each other to find the answers to our prayers.
9 x 12, 32 pp, Full-color illus., HC, 978-1-58023-080-3 **$16.95*** *For ages 4 & up*

How Does God Listen? *by Kay Lindahl; Full-color photos by Cynthia Maloney*
How do we know when God is listening to us? Children will find the answers to these questions as they engage their senses while the story unfolds, learning how God listens in the wind, waves, clouds, hot chocolate, perfume, our tears and our laughter.
10 x 8½, 32 pp, Full-color photos, Quality PB, 978-1-59473-084-9 **$8.99** *For ages 3–6*

In God's Hands *by Lawrence Kushner and Gary Schmidt; Full-color illus. by Matthew J. Baek*
9 x 12, 32 pp, Full-color illus., HC, 978-1-58023-224-1 **$16.99*** *For ages 5 & up*

In God's Name *by Sandy Eisenberg Sasso; Full-color illus. by Phoebe Stone*
Like an ancient myth in its poetic text and vibrant illustrations, this award-winning modern fable about the search for God's name celebrates the diversity and, at the same time, the unity of all the people of the world.
9 x 12, 32 pp, Full-color illus., HC, 978-1-879045-26-2 **$16.99*** *For ages 4 & up*

Also available in Spanish: El nombre de Dios
9 x 12, 32 pp, Full-color illus., HC, 978-1-893361-63-8 **$16.95**

In Our Image: God's First Creatures
by Nancy Sohn Swartz; Full-color illus. by Melanie Hall
A playful new twist on the Genesis story—from the perspective of the animals. Celebrates the interconnectedness of nature and the harmony of all living things.
9 x 12, 32 pp, Full-color illus., HC, 978-1-879045-99-6 **$16.95*** *For ages 4 & up*

Noah's Wife: The Story of Naamah
by Sandy Eisenberg Sasso; Full-color illus. by Bethanne Andersen
Opens young readers' religious imaginations to new ideas about the well-known story of the Flood. When God tells Noah to bring the animals of the world onto the ark, God also calls on Naamah, Noah's wife, to save each plant on Earth.
9 x 12, 32 pp, Full-color illus., HC, 978-1-58023-134-3 **$16.95*** *For ages 4 & up*

Also available: Naamah: Noah's Wife (A Board Book)
by Sandy Eisenberg Sasso; Full-color illus. by Bethanne Andersen
5 x 5, 24 pp, Full-color illus., Board Book, 978-1-893361-56-0 **$7.95** *For ages 0–4*

Where Does God Live? *by August Gold and Matthew J. Perlman*
Helps children and their parents find God in the world around us with simple, practical examples children can relate to.
10 x 8½, 32 pp, Full-color photos, Quality PB, 978-1-893361-39-3 **$8.99** *For ages 3–6*

* A book from Jewish Lights, SkyLight Paths' sister imprint

Women's Interest

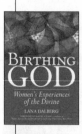

Birthing God: Women's Experiences of the Divine
By Lana Dalberg; Foreword by Kathe Schaaf
Powerful narratives of suffering, love and hope that inspire both personal and collective transformation.   6 x 9, 304 pp, Quality PB, 978-1-59473-480-9 **$18.99**

On the Chocolate Trail: A Delicious Adventure Connecting Jews, Religions, History, Travel, Rituals and Recipes to the Magic of Cacao
By Rabbi Deborah R. Prinz
Take a delectable journey through the religious history of chocolate—a real treat!
6 x 9, 272 pp, 20+ b/w photographs, Quality PB, 978-1-58023-487-0 **$18.99***

Women, Spirituality and Transformative Leadership
Where Grace Meets Power
Edited by Kathe Schaaf, Kay Lindahl, Kathleen S. Hurty, PhD, and Reverend Guo Cheen
A dynamic conversation on the power of women's spiritual leadership and its emerging patterns of transformation.   6 x 9, 288 pp, HC, 978-1-59473-313-0 **$24.99**

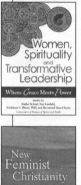

Spiritually Healthy Divorce: Navigating Disruption with Insight & Hope
By Carolyne Call   A spiritual map to help you move through the twists and turns of divorce.   6 x 9, 224 pp, Quality PB, 978-1-59473-288-1 **$16.99**

New Feminist Christianity: Many Voices, Many Views
Edited by Mary E. Hunt and Diann L. Neu
Insights from ministers and theologians, activists and leaders, artists and liturgists who are shaping the future. Taken together, their voices offer a starting point for building new models of religious life and worship.
6 x 9, 384 pp, Quality PB, 978-1-59473-435-9 **$19.99**; HC, 978-1-59473-285-0 **$24.99**

Bread, Body, Spirit: Finding the Sacred in Food
Edited and with Introductions by Alice Peck   6 x 9, 224 pp, Quality PB, 978-1-59473-242-3 **$19.99**

Dance—The Sacred Art: The Joy of Movement as a Spiritual Practice
By Cynthia Winton-Henry   5½ x 8½, 224 pp, Quality PB, 978-1-59473-268-3 **$16.99**

Daughters of the Desert: Stories of Remarkable Women from Christian, Jewish and Muslim Traditions
By Claire Rudolf Murphy, Meghan Nuttall Sayres, Mary Cronk Farrell, Sarah Conover and Betsy Wharton
5½ x 8½, 192 pp, Illus., Quality PB, 978-1-59473-106-8 **$14.99** Inc. reader's discussion guide

The Divine Feminine in Biblical Wisdom Literature
Selections Annotated & Explained
Translation & Annotation by Rabbi Rami Shapiro; Foreword by Rev. Cynthia Bourgeault, PhD
5½ x 8½, 240 pp, Quality PB, 978-1-59473-109-9 **$16.99**

Divining the Body: Reclaim the Holiness of Your Physical Self
By Jan Phillips   8 x 8, 256 pp, Quality PB, 978-1-59473-080-1 **$18.99**

Honoring Motherhood: Prayers, Ceremonies & Blessings
Edited and with Introductions by Lynn L. Caruso
5 x 7¼, 272 pp, Quality PB, 978-1-58473-384-0 **$9.99**; HC, 978-1-59473-239-3 **$19.99**

Next to Godliness: Finding the Sacred in Housekeeping
Edited by Alice Peck   6 x 9, 224 pp, Quality PB, 978-1-59473-214-0 **$19.99**

ReVisions: Seeing Torah through a Feminist Lens
By Rabbi Elyse Goldstein   5½ x 8½, 224 pp, Quality PB, 978-1-58023-117-6 **$16.95***

The Triumph of Eve & Other Subversive Bible Tales
By Matt Biers-Ariel   5½ x 8½, 192 pp, Quality PB, 978-1-59473-176-1 **$14.99**

White Fire: A Portrait of Women Spiritual Leaders in America
By Malka Drucker; Photos by Gay Block   7 x 10, 320 pp, b/w photos, HC, 978-1-893361-64-5 **$24.95**

Woman Spirit Awakening in Nature: Growing Into the Fullness of Who You Are
By Nancy Barrett Chickerneo, PhD; Foreword by Eileen Fisher
8 x 8, 224 pp, b/w illus., Quality PB, 978-1-59473-250-8 **$16.99**

Women of Color Pray: Voices of Strength, Faith, Healing, Hope and Courage
Edited and with Introductions by Christal M. Jackson
5 x 7¼, 208 pp, Quality PB, 978-1-59473-077-1 **$15.99**

* A book from Jewish Lights, SkyLight Paths' sister imprint